TELLING THE TRUTHINESS:

The Gospel According to Stephen Colbert

TELLING THE TRUTHINESS:

The Gospel According to Stephen Colbert

Richard Braaksma

Chapter Eight Press

Telling The Truthiness: The Gospel According to Stephen Colbert
© 2014 Richard Braaksma

Chapter Eight Press
3 Gateway Drive SW
Calgary, AB, Canada   T3E 4J8

Printed in the United States of America

Braaksma, Richard.
Telling The Truthiness: The Gospel According to Stephen Colbert.
ISBN 978-0-9939733-0-7
1. Religion —General. 2. Christianity —Theology. 3. Faith and Culture—Christianity.
First Edition
17 16 15 14 / 10 9 8 7 6 5 4 3 2 1

CONTENTS

ACKNOWLEDGMENTS

This book was a good idea that I never would have finished. Then in April 2014, CBS made the announcement that Stephen Colbert would succeed David Letterman on *The Late Show* in 2015. Shortly after came the announcement that *The Colbert Report* would wrap up in December, 2014.

I got to work and this is the result.

Thank you Sheri Braaksma for your support, ideas, love, and reading. You're my executive producer in all things. Thanks David Drury for being the first to like this idea three years ago and spurring me on. Thank you Rafael Alvarez for being a good writer and painstakingly nudging me to be better (alvarezfiction.com). Thank you Greg Daniel for your work, encouragement, and good advice. Thanks also to Jon Sweeney, Dallas Jenkins, Dan Balow for caring enough to give referrals and direction. Thanks Hillside Community Church for being a place where I can think freely, experiment, and wrestle with ideas. This project is me attempting to be "on mission."

Thanks friends and family for your encouragement (you're writing a book about *what?*).

Credit goes to Manoj for the caricature of Stephen Colbert on the cover (fiverr.com/manoms). Credit for the cover and back design goes to Bajon and crew (fiverr.com/pixelstudio) - excellent work.

Thanks Stephen Colbert! Thanks funny people and faithful people everywhere who make this world a better place.

1.

Truthiness and The Gospel According to Stephen Colbert

> Thomas said to him, "Lord, we don't know where you are going, how can we know the way?" Jesus answered, "I am the Way, the Truthiness, and the Life. No one comes to the Father except through me."
>
> John 14:5-6 (modified)[1]

THE GOSPEL TRUTHINESS

Yea, verily.

The idea for this book came to me after seeing a Facebook post circulating a Stephen Colbert quote under the heading "Organized Religion." The quote was from "The Wørd" segment of the December 16, 2010 episode of *The Colbert Report* leading up to Christmas:

---

[1] John 14:5-6, *The New International Version*. (2011). Grand Rapids, MI: Zondervan

"If this is going to be a Christian nation that doesn't help the poor, either we have to pretend that Jesus was just as selfish as we are, or we've got to acknowledge that He commanded us to love the poor and serve the needy without condition and then admit that we just don't want to do it."[2]

I had seen the episode, of course, and remembered reveling in its prophetic glory. If you haven't seen it, look it up.

The quote is even better in context, served up with Colbert's signature satirical delivery. Nevertheless, it stands on its own as indicated by its "going viral." It struck me as strange, however, that this statement was memed out over the "inter-webs" as an indictment of "organized religion."

Organized religion can, should, and does get its fair share of skewering from Colbert. But this quote was no fluffy "organized religion" joke. This was a statement about God and humanity, sin and righteousness, life and hypocrisy. This was about the light of truth uncovered and allowed to shine by the last thing you would have expected... truthiness.

TRUTHINESS

For the uninitiated, "truthiness" is a word coined by Colbert himself in the 2005 pilot of *The Colbert Report*.[3] Its definition has to do with the gut level affirmation and embrace of a worldview irrespective of the facts or reality because... it

---

[2] *The Colbert Report,* Comedy Central, Episode 813, aired December 16, 2010
[3] Episode 1, aired October 17, 2005

seems right, it feels right, and doggone it, it should be right so I affirm it wholeheartedly!

Truthiness constitutes the very character of the pundit Stephen Colbert and is the air *The Colbert Report* breathes deeply. But who is Stephen Colbert that we should be mindful of him? And what is this show with two silent t's?

The Colbert Report is a half hour "Fake News" show that has run for close to ten years on Comedy Central doing as many as 160 episodes a year. The center of the show is Stephen Colbert, the character – not to be confused with the husband, dad, comedian, and sometimes Sunday School teacher of the same name. Stephen's character is an over-the-top conservative news pundit modelled in part after Fox News' Bill O'Reilly, or "Papa Bear," as he is called on the show.

The character was experimentally developed in the eight years prior to the launch of *The Report* while Colbert was a correspondent on *The Daily Show with Jon Stewart*. In talking about Colbert the character, Colbert the comedian describes him as a "well intentioned, poorly informed, high status idiot."[4]

To avoid confusion, in these pages I will refer to Stephen Colbert the actor as "Stephen Colbert," but I will refer to Stephen Colbert the comedian as "Stephen Colbert." Sound good? In fact, it is often the ambiguity itself which makes the character work as a character and is an essential component of the actor's comedic craft.

---

[4] Colbert has repeated this shorthand description for his character in a plethora of interviews, for example, in an interview with Morley Safer on *60 Minutes* aired April 30, 2006.

One of the most surprising aspects of *The Colbert Report* is the staying power of Colbert's character year after year. Stephen's ability to stay in character (mostly) is remarkable. On rare occasions, slight breaks (the inability to keep a straight face, a sly smile) expose cracks in the façade but these only serve to enhance the comedy. Even then, the character is never dropped, always maintained.

Through news stories, ridiculous bits and sketches, interviews with pop stars and presidents, singing songs, participating in rallies and public appearances outside the show, testifying before Congress – the character does it all. One show, with one central sketch, and one central character has continued to captivate audiences, bring laughs, and win awards for well north of a thousand episodes.

The show has featured everything (and I mean everything) from poop jokes to fine points of theological discourse. Its brilliance, however, is that through consistent fakery it heightens awareness of reality. By staging everything it gives the viewer glimpses of un-staged authenticity. By a display of insanity it holds up a mirror to an insane world, taking aim at popular culture, politics, the media, nationalism, religion, ethics, and everything between.

This is how "truthiness" abounds.

Colbert commented, "Truthiness is a word I pulled right out of my keister..."[5]

He has also identified it as the "thesis" of his show. The thesis of this book, meanwhile, is that the comedic work of

---

[5] Episode 33, aired January 9, 2006

Stephen Colbert – in and through *The Colbert Report* and the character who shares his name – is a powerful, prophetic, and impactful voice of truth. Stephen Colbert embodies "truthiness" to show a "truthy" world their need for truth.

The Gospel Truthiness, served up hot by Stephen Colbert.

GOSPEL

But what is the gospel? There are few better questions. I'll take two stabs at it.

First, gospel is a genre of literature which addresses itself to the story of Jesus and why it matters. Second, gospel is a word that means "good news" and, also, usually has the story and person of Jesus as its primary referent.

When New Testament scholars hear the word "gospel," the first thing they think of is Matthew, Mark, Luke, and John – the first four books in the Christian canon. The proper titles of these books are "The Gospel According to Matthew," "The Gospel According to Mark," etc. But, when these books were written they had no titles at all. Actually, they weren't even books. They were written on papyrus scrolls and did not have chapter numbers, verse numbers, and they certainly did not have topical paragraph headings.

None of the gospels have an internal indication of authorship. Their titles were assigned later based on extra-biblical sources such as early church tradition. Mark isn't mentioned in "Mark." Luke isn't mentioned in "Luke." There are a few "Johns" in John but which one wrote it?

Johns are a dime a dozen – even today.

You don't go reading Matthew to hear the story of a guy named Matthew. You read Matthew because it is an account of Jesus and an argument for why it amounts to good news. This is also the case with the later gospels supposedly "according to" Thomas, Peter, Judas, and others.

In not-quite-as-pure fashion, *Telling the Truthiness: The Gospel According to Stephen Colbert* is not strictly all about Stephen Colbert. This book is not a biography. This is not an attempt to discover or uncover the "real" Stephen Colbert or chronicle his early life, his acting history, and all the nuances that have gone into his expertly crafted "character." Examining Stephen Colbert's gospel is simply about taking delight in the Truth behind the truthiness – reaching past Fox News into the Fake News to take joy in the Good News.

This brings me to the second meaning. The word gospel means "good news." The Greek is ευαγγελιον. The important thing to note is that the subject matter of the "gospels" and the definition of "gospel" are connected. The story of Jesus is associated with good news. The story of Jesus *is* The Good News.

In what sense? Because it's about heaven after we die? Like when Colbert declared the smudge on his forehead from an Ash Wednesday service was like a "club stamp" for "Club Heaven?" Or when he said he wanted a refund on his Catholicism after Jesuit Father Jim Martin declared that even atheists are redeemed?

No. The story of Jesus isn't good news because of what it reveals about us, but because of what it reveals about God.

Jesus reveals who God is. Jesus reveals that God is *for* peace, justice, wholeness, harmony, love, forgiveness, compassion, and selflessness.

Jesus reveals that God is on the side of the poor, he loves creation, he speaks truth to power, he befriends the weak, the outcast, and the "sinner." Jesus reveals that the least, lost, and little – even a state executed Jew rejected by tribe, political system, family, and friends – has a future in the life of God.

Jesus reveals that God identifies with the literal and metaphorical cross-bearers of the world and proclaims on them love, hope, and vindication in God. Jesus reveals that God is for us and not against us, even you and me. That's good news. That's gospel!

But Stephen Colbert?

If you were able to read the Greek word above, ευαγγελιον, it's where we get the English word "evangelist" which basically means "bearer of good news." Appropriately, New Testament scholars routinely refer to the gospel authors as "evangelists."

An evangelist is one who tells the Jesus story. An evangelist is a bearer of good news. I'm repeating myself to prevent confusion. A good deal of people in our culture proudly wear the title "evangelist" and use it as a vehicle to deliver bad news, like, "You're going to hell!"

They are on TV, too.

Let's retrace the logic. A gospel ("good news") is an account of Jesus. The story / person of Jesus is "good news" (gospel).

An evangelist is a gospel author, specifically, or more generally, a bearer of good news.   Good so far?

Well… in what parallel universe could Stephen Colbert be identified as an evangelist?

WHAT WOULD STEPHEN DO (W.W.S.D.)?

Through slanted speech, sarcasm, comedy, and mockery Stephen Colbert calls into question the beliefs and comfortable assumptions we hold dear.   In doing so, he opens the door of possibility to faith in something greater.

Stephen Colbert is no Savior of the world, but he may be more parts Messiah than anti-Christ.

When Jesus came on the scene he annoyed and perplexed a lot of people.   He turned social perceptions on their head, overturning tables as well as traditions.   The people he annoyed most were the religious, the politically powerful, and the rich (categories often blurred together).   He single-handedly made the neutral term "hypocrite" into a negative term referring to a person who represents one thing while being another.   Before Jesus, the word "hypocrite" simply meant "actor."   It was a theatre word.

Through "theatre" and mimicry, Stephen Colbert holds a mirror to culture.   His embodiment of truthiness and embracing inauthenticity exposes the truthiness and inauthenticity of the world around him.   Fittingly, he has often drawn harsh criticism from the religious, politically powerful, and the rich.

In the comedy of Stephen Colbert, mockery laced with love instead of soaked in cynicism make room for Good News in the middle of a Bad News world. This shouldn't surprise us, gospel is always birthed in the place people least expect it. Let's draw the parallel further and go to the first Christmas, some two thousand years ago.

What was happening in the world? Greco-Roman culture was flourishing. Caesar was reigning on the throne of the most powerful empire the world had ever known. Herod had beautified the Jewish Temple in Jerusalem. Elsewhere in the world, really important stuff was also happening. In China, for example, scientists were observing and recording sunspots, and inventing hydraulic powered bellows.

Christian Scripture makes the scandalous claim that the really important thing happening that Christmas involved an un-married Jewish teenager going into labor in a dirty barn behind a hotel. Appearances can be deceiving.

Truth shows up where you least expect it.

Even on a late night comedy show aired on a network known for its crassness and irreverence. In the eatery that is cable television, Comedy Central is typically considered more like a barn house trough then a fine dining establishment.

It may be a trough that cradles *The Colbert Report*, but like the trough that cradled the baby Jesus, there is glory there if you look for it. It is from that lowly place where night after night, with passionate buffoonery, robust lies, and ridiculous sub-narratives, Stephen Colbert invites us to question every-thing we've held dear, laugh at our deepest held beliefs, and see ourselves for who we are. And open the door for truth.

Away in a manger, no major network for a bed, *The Colbert Report* has turned the world on its head. The impact has not been a critique of "organized religion." It's far more subversive than that. Subversive like gospel.

In 2014, Colbert wraps up more than nine years at Comedy Central to take to the big leagues of late night network television. What will happen to the character and what measure of success will come in this new adventure in comedy? All this is yet to be seen. Undeniably, however, Colbert's last decade has been a cultural force with staggering impact. Come what may, Colbert's gospel has earned its hearing – truthiness speaking truth.

2.

Comedy is King

"A cheerful heart is a good medicine, but a downcast spirit dries up the bones."

Proverbs 17:22[1]

HE SAID WHAT?

Stephen Colbert has repeatedly advocated, implied, or declared the following:

• America should build an armed fence (or flaming moat) around its border to keep out "illegals."

• "The Gays" threaten the very fabric of America if not the world.

• Racism is not worth discussing because racism is "over."

---

[1] Proverbs 17:22 *The Holy Bible: New Revised Standard Version.* (1989). Nashville: Thomas Nelson Publishers.

• Helping the poor is best accomplished by the pursuit of greed and corporatization.

• God can be characterized as distant, impossible to please, angry, nonchalant in consigning people to hell and, above all, American.   Not only American, but precisely equivalent to the values and interests of America.

Stephen Colbert has propagated stereotypes of African Americans, Asians (thanks to his "Ching Chong Ding Dong" character), Hispanics, Catholics, Protestants, Muslims, welfare recipients, the LGBT community, scientists, atheists, poor, rich, conservatives, liberals, and Jesus.

In well over a thousand programs he has represented countless ignorant, offensive, insensitive, and flat out incorrect statements as right, factual, and gospel truth.

This is gospel?

Yes.   Explained in a single word: Comedy.

Simply applying the label "comedy," "satire," "irony," or "fake-newsery" is not all it takes to get a hall pass for being duplicitous, inauthentic, or offensive.   Comedy is a vocation that carries great responsibility.

When critics like Conservapedia bash Colbert as "unserious" they miss the point.[2] Being ridiculous, exaggerated, and obviously hypocritical with express comedic intention is profoundly serious.   This is true despite what comedians themselves may say.

---

[2] Conservapedia website entry on "Stephen Colbert"   URL:
www.conservapedia.com/Stephen_Colbert

Stephen Colbert and his mentor/friend/progenitor Jon Stewart often downplay the weightiness of their vocational identity.   In an interview at Harvard University Colbert quipped, "I'm a comedian from stem to stern. You can cut me open and count the rings of jokes."[3]   In this way Colbert and Stewart sometimes shirk or deflect attempts to amplify their status as prophets, truth-tellers, or agents of social change. They shrug and retreat, claiming to be "just" comedians.

They are wrong.   There is no "mere" anything.   It's like your mother saying, "I'm "just" a homemaker" or any other person downplaying their calling.   Many are called but few are chosen.   If you are called to be a homemaker, own it!   It's wondrous and significant.   If you are called to be a fool — for Christ, America, or Albania — own that, too!

We will develop questions of the Comic's vocation below. For now, though, what of their craft?   What about Comedy itself?   What about satire and the genre of Fake News in particular?

GENRE

Genre is a crucial matter in every field.   Consider the study of ancient Scripture as a point of entry.   Without inquiries about genre, context, and form of speech — even the smartest Bible interpreters are destined to flounder.

---

[3] "A Conversation with: Stephen Colbert" at the John F. Kennedy Jr. Center at Harvard, December 1, 2006.   Posted on YouTube in seven parts by user "feattie" — part 1/7 was removed because of copyright violation claims by Viacom part 2/7 URL: https://www.youtube.com/watch?v=q5iGtGlTzi0

First is genre. Students and scholars must ask of their text, "What kind of document is this? Is it a court transcript? A poem? A political speech? A love letter?"

The answers change one's reading dramatically.

Let's say you want to read about the birth of Jesus. You can turn to Revelation chapter 12 and read about a woman clothed with the sun, wearing a crown of twelve stars, and sporting wings enabling her to fly. Meanwhile, a seven-headed red dragon lies in wait to eat her baby son as soon as it is born.

Was all this going on in Bethlehem? Is this really about the birth of Jesus?

Yes, it is! But it is decidedly not narrative history. It is an apocalyptic account, common in Apocalyptic Literature, where authors tend to be a little bit heavy handed with their metaphoric / imaginative use of language to make clear that the events being described have cosmic significance.

Genre matters.

Second is context. "Who is writing this? Who is receiving this? When was it written? Where was it written? Why was it written?"

Is it addressed to Vikings en route to war on the high seas? Is it from a political prisoner exiled on an ancient island? Does it assume knowledge of first century Jewish religion and ritual? Or is it written to cynical postmodern North Americans who routinely assume that advertisers and politicians are liars?

Maybe you read in Scripture, "God sends his rain on the just and the unjust alike." If you live in 21st century Seattle you might interpret this negatively.

"Great! That settles it. God hates us all!"

However, if you lived in Ancient Israel where rain was the promise of good crops and the sign of God's favor... The same text would take on a very different flavor.

Context matters.

Third is form of speech. "Is this written to a lover? Is it 'off the cuff' or are the news cameras rolling? Is it a grocery list or military instructions?"

Failing to ask these questions can result in strange interpretations. Let's say you read Genesis 1 as a blow by blow literal-sequential account of God's creation later spoken verbatim by the same Creator to Moses. Reading the text like that might cause you to jump to the conclusion that the world is only 6,000 years old and dinosaur bones are a test of faith planted by the devil!

Not only that, such a reading might render it difficult for you to appreciate features in the text such as the imbedded polemic against Egyptian or Babylonian creation myths; or the fascinating poetic structure wherein days one, two, and three provide the "form" which are then filled in by the "content" of days four, five, and six.

Observations such as these might seem threatening. But only if genre, context, and form of speech are not taken seriously.

How do questions of genre inform us in interpreting *The Colbert Report*?

COMEDY IS KING

"Laughter is the best medicine," say the sages.

The sages, in this case, have been backed up by modern science and medicine.

Studies of every kind proclaim that laughter makes you healthier, happier, live longer, and be more productive. Just Google it. LOL! LMAO!

They also say that it takes less facial muscle power to smile than it does to frown. This, however, I don't believe. I effortlessly frown all day still remember the pain in my face at the end of my wedding day after so many smiling poses…

I digress. Laughter is good for you. Comedy is great. Why?

Comedy allows us to exit our dogmatic frameworks and look back at our lives, our constructs, and our understanding of reality from a different point of view. Comedy is one of the few mechanisms that grant us this sense of transcendence – to take all the things we cling to passionately and hold dear, juggle them loosely, and observe how they react.

Comedy allows us to face our hypocrisy, the other side of the argument, and our typical human charade whereby we act like we have all things figured out.

Comedy exposes the gap between our professed beliefs and how those beliefs operate. For example, almost everyone I know is wise enough to know and believe deep down in their soul that money cannot buy happiness.   Engaging in relationships, family, and love is far richer and more rewarding than being obsessed with material possessions. Nevertheless, almost everyone I know in our culture (at least to some extent) lives their lives in such a way that betrays these beliefs.

It is not necessarily disingenuous.   We do this without thinking.   It is easy to decry the evils of oil production while driving a super SUV to our kid's soccer practice or consuming our mineral water and organic tofu in oil produced plastics. There is a gap between what we profess to believe and how those beliefs operate.

The gap is funny.   We all know the gap exists but only comedy allows us to expose and address it.

Comedy can be a catalyst whereby we transform into more authentic people.   Comedy enables us to face the darkness in the world but also as it exists in ourselves.   Racial humor and stereotypes expose the racism and prejudice of the progressive and the "backwoods" alike.

Sexual humor allows us a space to bring out an aspect of human existence that is both compelling and mysteriously always beyond our understanding.   Stand-up routines take everyday living and show us the absurdity and fickle nature of it all.

Comedy allows us to face our fears and at the same time dispels fear.   On "Meet the Press," Colbert pointed out it is impossible to be afraid when you are laughing.   He qualified, "That's not a philosophical statement... it's a physiological statement. When you laugh, you're not afraid."[4]

In a world driven by fear, comedy is a release valve.

Just consider the daily television news on which *The Colbert Report* is an endless riff.   The news, regardless of channel or network, is nothing short of a fear orgy.   Fear of terrorists, fear of economic collapse, fear of weather, fear of disease, fear of local crime, fear of identity theft, fear of immigrants, fear of killer bees, killer dogs, and, of course, bears.[5]

Comedy is therapy.   It puts us in the chair where we can hash out our fears, quit repressing them, and get them out in the open where they have to be dealt with.   And then laugh at them.

In this sense, comedy is nothing short of angelic.

In Scripture, what is the first thing angels and God always speak to human beings at the time of their visitation?

"Do not be afraid!"[6]

John the Elder puts it this way: "Perfect love casts out fear."[7]

---

[4] *Meet the Press (TAKE TWO: msnbc.com)* with Tim Russert online exclusive aired October 21, 2007.   URL: http://www.nbcnews.com/video/meet-the-press/21400561#21400561

[5] For interesting backstory information on Stephen Colbert's fear of bears on *The Colbert Report* see "The Playboy Interview: Stephen Colbert on Politics, Grief, and Bill O'Reilly" by Eric Spitznagel on April 10, 2014.   URL: http://playboysfw.kinja.com/the-playboy-interview-stephen-colbert-on-politics-gri-1561831379

[6] For example, Genesis 15:1, 21:17, 26:24, 35:17; Isaiah 41:10, Matthew 14:7, 28:5, 28:10; Mark 6:50; Luke 1:13; 1:30, 2:10; John 6:20; Acts 1:9, 27:24, Revelation 1:17

It is a beautiful picture: Love itself operative in our laughter.

ON THE DARK SIDE

Comedy can also be used for evil.   Any school child knows that jokes can be packed with vitriol and cruelty.   Adults know it, too.   When a mean joke is delivered effectively, it packs more hurt than a punch.

Sticks and stones.

Comedy's practitioners (from professional comedians to the average Joe making a crack at the dinner table) face the same temptation – going for the cheap, "mean" laugh.

The book of James pointed out some two thousand years ago (in somewhat comical hyperbolic fashion) that words can build up or tear down.   James called the tongue a wild beast and a blazing fire, unique among creation in its wild, powerful, and untameable nature.[8]

The danger of humor is related to the dark side that is present in most of our base, human institutions.   Like ritual.   Ritual and habit can remind us who we are, shape us, and train us in the same way that exercise trains an athlete.   Or, ritual can draw lines that allow us to divide, alienate, and persecute people who are not like us.   It can create the illusion of sub-classes of humanity and set up fictitious, monstrous "Others" to be feared and condemned.

---

[7] 1 John 4:18 *The Holy Bible: New Revised Standard Version.* (1989). Nashville: Thomas Nelson Publishers.
[8] See James 3:1-9

Comedy can do the same.

I will not claim that Colbert is incapable of crossing such lines from time to time.

Liberals and conservatives set each other up as "straw men" embraced or set up to fall at almost every level of political discourse in America.   Colbert is identifiably "left" and can be fairly accused of misrepresenting the "right" on numerous occasions.

Nevertheless, disagreement and dissent are not the same as "meanness."

At his best, Colbert's comedic orientation is noble. "I'm not an assassin," he has said in describing his interviewing style.[9]

Before every show he coaches his guests on how to get their point of view across, even when he disagrees with them, so they are not completely overwhelmed by his bold and brash character. Shaming and ridiculing people is never the goal.

TELL THE TRUTH

Funny can be an escape, but at its purest it is the exact opposite.   This, I argue, is the primary function of comedy. Comedy is truth telling.

---

[9] "Colbert: Re-Becoming the Nation We Always Were" on *Fresh Air* with Terry Gross on NPR.   URL: http://www.npr.org/2012/10/04/162304439/colbert-re-becoming-the-nation-we-always-were

Life is difficult. Life involves suffering. Human beings are complex creatures beautifully and wonderfully made yet complicit in the ills that surround us.

Laughing at ourselves and each other can tear down the facades and illusions we erect through the vilification of others. Laughing at ourselves enables us to see that we, mortal creatures under God, are in this thing together (whatever this "thing" is).

Colbert has credited his late mother with his "big picture" approach to comedy. Commenting on the tragic loss of his father and brothers at when he was ten, Colbert remarked in an interview with New York Times Magazine, "She taught me to be grateful for my life regardless of what that entailed, and that's directly related to the image of Christ on the cross and the example of sacrifice that he gave us. What she taught me is that the deliverance God offers you from pain is not; no pain — it's that the pain is actually a gift. What's the option? God doesn't really give you another choice."[10]

Running from the darkness is bad comedy. Wrestling it like Jacob wrestled the angel is where the power lays – the power of truth. Perceiving, sometimes in ways that are difficult to describe, that the lines we've drawn hard and fast in our own consciousness may not be as hard and fast as we thought.

That revelation gives us joy and hope. Hope because maybe the lines that divide us on the one hand and restrain and bind

[10] "How Many Stephen Colbert's Are There?" by Charles McGrath, The New York Times Magazine, published January 4, 2012. URL: http://www.nytimes.com/2012/01/08/magazine/stephen-colbert.html?ref=magazine&_r=0

us on the other are imaginary.   Maybe they are constructs in need of rebuilding and reframing.

The first step to realizing it might well be an earthquake of laughter to shake our structures down.

3.

Fake News and the Sins of the World

Hypocrites! You know how to interpret the appearance of the earth
and the sky. How is it that you don't know how to interpret this
present time?

Luke 12:56[1]

LIGHTS, CAMERA...

Red, white, and blue light take form as stars and stripes burst-
ing into my living room from my 90" flat screen TV. I sit
bracing myself – clutching the armrests of my club chair.

A proud bald eagle feathered with America's flag flaps, soars,
and dives. Fast paced and confident "news music" gallops
through my home theater speakers.

---

[1] Luke 12:56 *The New International Version*. (2011). Grand Rapids, MI:
Zondervan

Behold!   The pundit stands like a god among men.   His suit is perfect.   His hair is perfect.   He grins wryly, raises an eyebrow, and stretches out his hand.

Where is he standing?   Is he in heaven?

No time to speculate!   Now he is running.   The cosmic man. Part Messiah, part hero, and part savior.   He's running.   This confident warrior through a jungle of words.

Turning words, twirling words.   They are his words.   Words he wields.   Words that make him:

"Self-evident," "smartyr," "bold," "essential," "kingmaker," "patriot," "sponsored," "influential," "sanctified," "paid-triot," "courageous."

Without breaking stride he grabs Old Glory.   He leaps and begins to descend to earth.   Ah! Gloriously behold his angelic descent   through   all   these   words,   still   turning,   forming   a tornado around him to assist him, define him, and serve him:

"Honorable,"   "chiseled,"   "invincible,"   "strong,"   "high-fructose,"   "institutional,"   "passionate,"   "authoritative," "national   treasure,"   "powerful,"   "originalist,"   "sponsored," "indivisible,"   "all-beef,"   "principled,"   "worthy," "constitutional,"   "tallish,"   "love   me,"   "independent," "fearless," "enlarged," "confident."

He lands squarely at center stage.   Of where?

Is this the center of the universe?   Yes.   It must be.   He plants the flag like a superhero – fearless, bold, and triumphal. In this act, the victory of Iwo Jima, Neil Armstrong on the moon, and the first ascent of Everest are all rolled into one.

From the epicenter of this heroic flag plant, atomic ripples spread across the stage and throughout the cosmos. It is too much to take, too radiant.

Mercifully, the camera backs off and zooms out to a wide shot revealing stadium citadels. This is the world's stage, the stadium of all being, shaped as a giant letter "C." Colbert looks me in the eye with a steely gaze. Then the banner appears – like a beacon of hope in a vast wilderness or a sign on a map that says, "You are here."

What does it say? "The Colbert Report."

I've been told. I've been located. I have arrived where I need to be. My whole life has led up to this point.

Before I can catch my breath... the eagle shrieks. It's as though my very soul is in its talons. The last round of music commences as stage lights appear. The camera pans the audience and arrives at the desk where meaning will be restored and all my questions will be answered. There sits Stephen Colbert.

The audience is screaming, cheering, and chanting, "Stephen, Stephen." They used to chant "U.S.A, U.S.A" but audiences evolve and now they realize "Stephen" is simply the personal name and obvious expression for all that is "U.S.A."

After allowing just a little too much cheering, the anchor quiets the crowd, "Nation, nation..." That's how he addresses us. We are included. We belong. We are his.

And now it begins. My brain is checked out. My gut has checked in. Stephen Colbert leans into the desk toward the front facing camera and I am ready for the next 22 minutes.

To be told what I care about, what I'm angry about, my health concerns, my entertainment preferences, my religious sensibilities, and, of course, my political viewpoints.

I AM THE SUN

Watching *The Report* is like being invited to play along in a grand game. The show opening and every subsequent moment follow the same narrative.   The desk, the stage, the library, and the entire set are all carefully placed components that create an air of infallibility and confidence.

Colbert pointed out, "There are no televisions behind me, like the way [*NBC Nightly News* anchor] Brian Williams has, or even [*Daily Show* host] Jon [Stewart]. At certain angles, there are monitors behind Jon that have the world going on, which implies that that's where the news is, and that's where the information is, and the person in front of it is the conduit through which this information is given to you. But on my set, I said, 'I don't want anything behind me, because I am the sun. It all comes from me. I'm not channeling anything. I *am* the source.'"[2]

The audience, meanwhile, is every bit a "character" as the pundit.   In the style of improv, Colbert characterizes any given show as one big scene.   Everything is effect. Everything is hyperbole.   The audience is "in on it."   So is every viewer tuned in on tablet or television.

---

[2] "Stephen Colbert" by Nathan Rabin.   AV Club interview, January 25, 2006.   URL: http://www.avclub.com/article/stephen-colbert-13970

In the Colbert universe, disbelief is not suspended so much as the suspension of disbelief is pretended.

This is Fake News.

FAKE NEWS

Fake News is a relatively recent phenomena.

Newspapers and radio have long featured sardonic and sarcastic pieces. Comedians have used "current events" as the launching point of their routines for ages. But sustained endeavors of engaging Fake News as the primary platform for TV comedy is much more recent.

TV news itself, as a genre, is the most serious TV programming we have. Making fun of the things we take most seriously is one of the easiest ways to be funny. As a culture that loves television, television news as a target for satire is obvious.

In 1962-63 the inspiring *That Was The Week That Was* or *TW3* satirized English politicians on television "across the pond." To a certain extent, this programme was the inspiration in the 1970s for *Saturday Night Live*, Canada's *SCTV*, and even *The Muppets* with Jim Henson as the voice of "The Newsman." These shows all entertained audiences with recurring segments that spoofed the news – demonstrating that the news "works" as a platform for improv and sketch comedy.

Only in the last twenty years, however, has this insight been milked for all its worth through the inception of shows like *The Daily Show, The Colbert Report,* as well as *This Hour Has 22 Minutes*

(Canada).[3]   These programs took the bet that faking the news would be funny enough to sustain for more than just a segment.   The gamble has paid off.   For a network like Comedy Central, Fake News has been their longest running, highest rated meal ticket.

Jon Stewart took over *The Daily Show* from Craig Kilborn in 1999.   Stewart tweaked and transformed the show from a parade of pop-culture parody into a more sophisticated critique involving politics, world headlines, and particularly the shortcomings of major news media outlets.   That is, of course, if you can classify a program that liberally engages in sexual innuendo and scatological jokes as "sophisticated."

The Daily Show (or *The Colbert Report's* "Old Testament" as I like to call it) features Jon Stewart (Moses?) overseeing the show, observing the news, and pointing out what is comical and ridiculous in the "real" news.   The central joke of the opening monologue usually involves observing what the major news media paid obscene amounts of attention to or, conversely, what it conspicuously failed to cover.

The effect on the viewer is to look back at the "real" news and think, "I can't believe we actually live in a world where this is what passes for news and serious discourse!"   Jon Stewart is aghast, incredulous.   We join him in his incredulity.

Stewart, though, is a straight man.   He is not a character.   To be sure, Stewart uses overplayed reactions, mock disbelief, emotional break downs, and freak outs as well as any comic. But he does so like a dad at the dinner table who can break into

---

[3] This list could include the UK's *Spitting Image* which had a successful twelve year run from 1984-1996 using puppets instead of people to satirize English politics.

a story, imitate an accent, or sing a song while no one loses track of who he really is or what he is about.

In between the "straight" observational monologue and the typical-night-time-talk-show-promotional-interview at the end of the show, *The Daily Show* makes room for any manner of over the top segments involving correspondents on assignment, wild sketches, mockumentary moments, or pretty much any sick and twisted thing (with a point) that the writers can imagine. It was as a Fake News correspondent in this middle portion that Stephen Colbert's "character" began to emerge.

While Stewart plays himself, Colbert does not. At The Grammys, public rallies, or appearances on each other's shows, whenever and wherever Stewart and Colbert perform together Stewart is the straight man while Colbert is the fool. Colbert can "dial down" his character very low when the moment or interview demands it, but it never gets turned off.

Comparing himself to Stewart, Colbert once likened Jon to the kid in the back of the class shooting spitballs. His own "shtick," he argued, is to be the spitball itself – hitting the target between the eyes in gobby, gooey glory.[4] Keeping with this metaphor, *The Colbert Report*, aka the "New Testament," was the "spitball" launched in 2005 as an offshoot of *The Daily Show*.

The Report is the supreme expression of Fake News. Its birth signified the further narrowing of categories to the highest degree of premium, unfiltered, pure fakery. Fake News as a

---

[4] "Talks at Google," Stephen Colbert interview with Eric Schmidt published December 14, 2012. URL: https://www.youtube.com/watch?v=-HpBHWUPa8Q

genre journeyed from sketch material within comedy shows, to the general ethos of *The Daily Show*, to a dedicated platform for Stephen Colbert to crank up the dial and insist that the grand act inform everything.

On *The Report*, the opening monologue is in character, the skits are in character, the typical-night-time-talk-show-promotional-interview that closes the show is in character. It is a lie from start to finish. And the only way to hear the truth is for the lie to be consistent, continuous, and uncompromising.

How is this possible? How is it that a lie reveals the truth better than simply telling the truth? Simple. We humans are a disingenuous people who can only confront our disingenuous selves when we are confronted with complete and utter hypocrisy. Oscar Wilde declared people are least truthful when they play it straight. "Give a man a mask and he will tell the truth."[5]

WE'RE ALL GOING TO HELL!

The trouble with the Good News is that it implies an already operative Bad News. To "get saved" means you need something to get saved from. As humans, we are aware that huge problems loom before us. Nevertheless, we consciously and subconsciously avoid confronting them head on. Like Jack Nicholson's character in A Few Good Men badgered by

---

[5] A quote widely credited to Oscar Wilde and in keeping with his famous essay *The Truth of Masks*

Tom Cruise on the stand we cry, "The truth?   The truth? You can't handle the truth![6]"

The truth is that we are all sinners complicit in the evils of the world.

Saying as much used to be the job of preachers.   Like the ones who would go from town to town hosting tent meeting revivals and letting everybody know we're on the highway to hell.   Nowadays, preachers have lost their credibility thanks to sex and money scandals and we're not sure *what* we believe about hell anymore.

We don't have the time of day to hear a slick haired preacher tell us we're sinners.   But we can take it from Stephen Colbert.

Yea, verily.   Fake News informs audiences that the world is sinful, broken, and in need of repentance.   And we're complicit in the whole business.

The Fake News warns us not to listen to the seductive words of Babylon and the powers that be – like the politicians and the newsmakers who want to lull and sedate us with the maddening wine of their idolatries.   Fake News shines a light on the world whose "way is wide and leadeth to destruction" and urges us toward the narrow path… though it is anything but straight.[7]

A basic assumption of the Judeo-Christian worldview is that creation is good, and yet at once sinful and corrupt.   To Sarah

---

[6] *A Few Good Men* (1992) directed by Rob Reiner, Columbia Pictures, Castle Rock Entertainment

[7] Matthew 7:13-14   *The Holy Bible: King James Version.* (2009). (Electronic Edition of the 1900 Authorized Version). Bellingham, WA: Logos Research Systems, Inc.

Palin, that means liberals exist.　For others, it is a little more complex than that.

Hopefully, most people also think that whatever the trouble with the world happens to be – it is something we should concern ourselves with addressing.　Whether we think that is best done by education, social evolution, scientific advancement, or the love of God we recognize that there are real "ills" and evils in the world – both systemic and localized.

Hopefully, we realize that we are not innocent.　Hopefully, we realize that the choices, values, lifestyle, and privilege we enjoy (right down to watching comedy programs on cable or writing about it) make us indirectly and sometimes directly complicit in the ills of the world.

If this is true, it is also true that it's difficult to know what to do about it.　How does a fish respond to a critique of water? The easiest response is denial – to function as if these problems simply don't exist or file them in some hard to reach spot in our minds.

It is amazing how easy it is to take oneself seriously while critiquing the evils of big corporations over a tasty latte at Starbucks.　I've done it!　But at least our guilt is assuaged by the few cents of that latte which "give back" and do something worthwhile elsewhere in the world (if it were a segment of The Wørd the commentary caption might read, "take a mile and give back an inch").

We *know* we're complicit.　We know we're hypocritical.　We care.　But it is hard to stare our own hypocrisy in the face and know what to do about.

Enter News de la Façade.   It has been said that more young people get their news from *The Daily Show* and Stephen Colbert then from the "real" news.   According to Fox News (and even Stewart and Colbert) this indicates a sad state of affairs.

I beg to differ.   The fake-maker newsmen get more laughs but are decidedly *not* less authentic.   Just because they're funny doesn't mean they aren't bearing witness to real ills in the world.

SOMETHING'S WRONG

So what's wrong with the world?   Fake News has covered a great deal.

Let's start with consumerism.   Product placement is present in all media but highlighted and parodied by Fake News.   The story?   We are consumers.   All of us.   Born and bred to seek pleasure, comfort, and products to make us complete.   Our consumerism results in poisonous side effects for the rest of the planet, but we shelter our consciousness and consciences.

What else have we seen on Fake News?

Sweatshops, misery imposed by mineral mining, AIDS, poverty, war, global violence, global warming, human trafficking, pollution, corruption... We know these exist. They are hard to look at for any amount of time without flinching.

But are we complicit?

How about what's going on in America?

Our police forces are becoming increasingly militarized and violent, our justice system is racially biased, our prisons are better populated than anywhere in the world (USA #1), and not only that, packing them has become lucratively profitable for Private Prisoneers.™ The middle class is disappearing, wealth disparity is reaching enormous proportions, the center of power is shifting (or has shifted) from Washington to Wall Street, and corporations are now "people" with unlimited rights of free speech to enable them to buy elections, form policy, all while ducking taxes by moving money offshore.

What else?

Banks and car companies are exempt from moral, ethical, and legal consequences because they are "too big to fail," Democrats and Republicans vilify each other, vilify constituents, vilify whoever they can to advance their own agendas. The privacy and rights of citizens are increasingly theoretical and ignored from the lowest to the highest branches of governments (thanks NSA!).

Debt is on the rise (individually and nationally), so is murder, identity theft, childhood obesity, homelessness, and unemployment... but *not* education!

Immigration policies and practices are not only racist, but hypocritical. Domestic violence, drunk driving, school shootings, mental un-health, bullying, animal cruelty, ignorance, un -fair hiring practices, non-domestic violence, and police profiling are all around us.

Scapegoating, fear mongering, and blaming people groups in sound-bytes increases domestically while drones threaten handfuls of terrorists and busloads of civilians around the world. Anything else? I don't know… our kids are on drugs and the greatest aspiration of our culture is to keep up with the Kardashians!

The world is a messed up place.

REAL NEWS - AN EYE FOR AN EYE

The world is a messed up place. And it's ours. We made it this way. We live in the world of our making. Whatever happens, we're to blame or to be praised.

The Fake News enables us to face this world and want to change it.

The real news, meanwhile, allows us to displace both the problems of the world and our responsibility for them. Typically, the "real" news casts its audience as serious, caring citizens. Like in the Fake News, our cares, concerns, and the appropriate response are provided for us.

According to the "real" news narrative, our primary concern should be the domestic issues that threaten our way of life. Preferably, these stories involve a scapegoat and villain from an "other" group, individual, or someone on the other side of the political spectrum.

In the news, violence in the world is bad and sad but the underlining reasons are rarely mined deeply or handled as important complexities for mass public consideration. How these "situations" threaten our way of life (national interest) or call for our involvement appears to be far more interesting than how our nation has been involved in the past, how we are perceived in the world, and whether there is any truth in those perceptions.

Of course, the news must also keep us afraid at all times.

Colbert names a segment of his show "The Threat Down" but the "real" news has been doing this kind of coverage far longer and far better. It is commonplace to spin fear of killer bees, fear of our neighbor, and fear of insidious diseases lurking in sofa cushions.

In the "real" news, natural disasters and crashes need to be covered and, where possible, blame should be assigned and heads should roll.

Weather is nice to know about (we have entire channels devoted to it), car chases are fun (especially if you live in Los Angeles), the DOW goes up and down but no mention of who's back it is breaking.

The "real" news also "keeps it real" by checking in with celebrities and highlighting entertainment stories. And whatever is being discussed, it is always delightful to have a forum where people argue and yell, talking over each other in person or on split screens.

Through all this, the "real" news sustains the myth that the world "out there" has turned bad while our assumptions and ideology remain intact. Our way of life is sustainable, free-dom and choice have to do with brand variety, happiness is held up by the twin pillars of comfort and security, violence is a legitimate response to violence, the systems we endorse uphold human rights and dignity above all.

It's difficult to describe water to a fish. The "water" we fish have trouble seeing is our own ideology.

Ideology unquestioned by "real" news is precisely what Fake News critiques and undermines. The way it does so is to undermine the prevailing ideology by saying the exact same thing and drawing it out to its extreme conclusions until we have to confess that something is broken.

Colbert's two books (he claims he shouted into a tape recorder) are supreme examples of this. By making an extended and celebratory case for "American Exceptionalism" he undermines the doctrine completely. The book titles say it all – *I Am America (And So Can You)* (2007), and *America Again: Re-Becoming the Greatness We Never Weren't* (2012).

Meanwhile, the "real" news more closely resembles the following quote from Colbert: "The present climate of the "world" by which I mean "America" is a crisis of worldviews and in this crisis of worldviews there is no neutral ground."

The problem is not with us. The problem is with them.

THEM

Demonizing the world "out there" is not only the tact of "real" news, it is also the tact of politicians and even fundamentalist churches. This is ironic in that the Bible's definition for this sort of thing is "spiritual blindness."

A great comic named Jesus once took the local pundits of his day to task calling them "blind guides" and "whitewashed tombs" who notice the speck of sawdust in the eyes of others but miss the 2x4 hanging off their own eyeballs. He also accused of them of straining out a gnat while willing to swallow a camel.

Hilarious.

The point is that the "sins of the world" I've listed or whatever else we might uncover or imagine – blindness is a sin greater still. Apathy or unwillingness to confront what we have created (or been co-opted into) is worse. As Cornel West once said on *The Colbert Report*, "Indifference to evil is more insidious than evil itself."[8]

Facing the darkness is something that comedy enables us to do. And it equips us for the task.

Exposing the world's evil while stripping it of its power through laughter – that is the strength of comedy. Satirical punditry takes it to a whole new level. When Stephen Colbert speaks falsely and hypocritically, we can confront our own falsehood and hypocrisy.

The Colbert Report is in this way a paradox. It raises issues and demands we take them seriously precisely by insisting we not be so serious. The mechanism is powerful. If we can avoid being sticks in the mud and go along for the ride for even 22 minutes; we can travel to the darkest depths of our world, our souls, and imaginations laughing all the way.

Comedy strips our claim to innocence right down to the bone. Repentance is a theological world that means "change your mind." Comedy critiques our ways of viewing ourselves, the

---

[8] Episode 626, aired on October 26, 2009

world, and God, but at the same time it ushers us to a place where renewed vision is possible and hope is meaningful.

4.

Prophets and Parables

The LORD said to Hosea, "Go! Take for yourself a wife of prostitution, and have children of prostitution, for the whole land is given to prostitution, forsaking the LORD."

Hosea 1:2[1]

ACTED PARABLES

The Great Prophet Isaiah had two sons. One was named, "The Remnant Shall Return" and the other "Spoil Quickly, Plunder Speedily."[2] Isaiah rang out some strange proclamations in his day, but it must have been equally strange for the neighborhood when Mrs. Isaiah rang the dinner bell and called from the front porch for the kids to come in.

As early as Isaiah in the 8th century BCE, comedy, exaggeration, and symbolic acts were being used to deliver prophetic

---

[1] Hosea 1:2, author's translation
[2] Isaiah 7:3, 8:3

messages to the larger society. Still... it's hard not to feel bad for Isaiah's kids. Bullies can be brutal.

Some folks in the Bible had it even worse. Ezekiel was instructed by God to lie on one side for the better part of a year and cook his food over human dung to "make a point" to God's people.[3] Hosea was called to take a prostitute for a wife to illustrate that Israel was unfaithful to God her "husband.[4]"

In the biblical narrative, funny names and weird, eccentric, symbolic acts (especially when sponsored by God) are called "acted parables" - actions which illustrate a societal ill or illuminate a theological truth.

Acted parables in Scripture are a primary mode of prophetic communication. The tradition continued all the way to Jesus. Riding into Jerusalem on a donkey, cursing a fig tree, washing his disciples feet – all of these were acted parables.[5]

One of the most famous of Jesus' stunts-with-a-purpose was the so-called "cleansing" of the Temple.[6] Forget the "meek and mild" stereotypes. Jesus took up a whip and drove out the money changers from the Jerusalem Temple; overturning tables and inciting a ruckus.

The gospel writers draw our attention to this because the action had purpose. Jesus' anti-establishment outburst had less to do with what the money changers were doing and more to do with the big picture of Jesus acting out God's judgment

---

[3] Ezekiel 4:12
[4] Hosea 1:2
[5] Mark 11:1-11, 11:12-25; John 13:1-17
[6] John 2:15; Matthew 21:12-17

against the Temple system and the powers which represented and maintained it.

In the biblical narrative, Jesus, Paul, and the first ever Christian martyr Stephen were all arrested for statements and actions perceived as "anti-Temple" and anti-establishment.[7]

And who is named after Stephen?   Lots of people, but one of them is Stephen Colbert.

SUPER PAC

Stephen Colbert is a master of acted parables.   He has continually attempted to "make a point" with over-the-top public antics.   Colbert formed a Super PAC, ran for president, worked alongside migrant workers in order to testify before Congress concerning Immigration Reform, staged a rally to Restore Sanity and/or Fear, had his head shaved on the orders of Barack Obama, "signed up" for military boot-camp, and much more.

Some acted parables are more effective than others, but their "function" is not so very different for Stephen Colbert than they were for the great biblical prophets.   In both cases, acted parables are about pulling off stunts that demand attention to a greater truth.

One poignant example drawn out by Colbert over the process of almost two years was the formation of Colbert Super PAC. In a historically developing piece of performance art, Colbert navigated federal election laws and formed a real world

---

[7] Matthew 26:65; Acts 6:13; Acts 21:28

organization to legally launder over a million dollars with the express purpose of materially influencing so-called democratic elections while protecting the anonymity of his financial backers.

The parable simultaneously educated audiences about election funding while demonstrating how the center of power in America has shifted away from Washington toward corporate and big money interests.   If money can't buy an election, it can certainly buy a lot of influence and power.

Colbert called his parable an "act of discovery" aimed to uncover "there is a whole political industrial complex that is not only raising money but that is built around making money off of the fact that there is so much money in politics."[8]   Here is how it worked:

During a show in early 2011, Colbert attempted to form a PAC (Political Action Committee) to pool money for political influence.   The bit evolved from an idea to make a parody commercial based on presidential hopeful Tim Pawlenty's television PAC ads soliciting funds.

It became an attempt to form an actual organization on air.

Colbert's antics faced their first roadblock when Comedy Central's parent company Viacom objected that Colbert's forming a PAC posed a conflict of interest based on regulations restricting PAC's cooperation with commun- ications and media outlets.   Not to be dissuaded, Colbert

---

[8] On *Meet the Press* with David Gregory on NBC, published October 14, 2012.   URL:
http://www.nbcnews.com/video/meet-the-press/49407301

consulted his lawyer (on air) and deftly ducked Viacom's objections by forming a Super PAC instead.

Unlike a regular PAC, a Super PAC could have no direct collusion with a given campaign (except through "media"). On the other hand, Super PAC's were completely exempt from campaign restrictions and could raise unlimited funds to advance their political agenda.

Before long, another problem presented itself. Colbert's Super PAC was not getting the support he anticipated. Potential donors, it seemed, were dissuaded from giving by the fact that the Super PAC was legally obligated to disclose the source of donations over two hundred dollars. Colbert modified his strategy again (playing it all out on national TV in segments of *The Colbert Report*).

Colbert's shift in strategy was to register a non-profit "shell" corporation in Delaware to legally receive heaps of cash from deep pockets who wanted to keep their identities hidden. The shell corporation could then pass those funds along to the Super PAC.

Signing forms and navigating legal issues were all TV moments hammed up for the viewing pleasure of the Colbert Nation. Stephen's lawyer Trevor Potter did guest spots on the show for every step of the journey.[9]   Potter, not incidentally, was also the chair of the Federal Election Committee and could attest to the legality of every shady move.

The official name for Stephen Colbert's Colbert Super PAC was "Americans for a Better Tomorrow, Tomorrow." The

---

[9] See episode 856, aired March 30, 2011 and subsequent episodes featuring Trevor Potter

name of the anonymous shell corporation was "Anonymous Shell Corporation" until it was changed to "Colbert Super PAC SHH Institute" with the stated aim of "educating the public."

Indeed it did!

Before dissolving the Super PAC in late 2012 (and giving almost a million dollars to actual charities like Donors Choose) the Colbert Super PAC ran attack ads accusing Mitt Romney of being a serial killer and encouraged / instructed college students how to form their own Super PAC.   The Super PAC was at one point signed over to Jon Stewart so it could sort-of-but-not-really support Stephen Colbert's campaign to be President of the United States in South Carolina.

The prophet Isaiah would have been proud.

The Super PAC, idiotic posturing, and showboating which surrounded this stunt turned a bright light on one very important aspect of political corruption.   Colbert insisted that *everything* be done in complete congruity with the law.   This made it that much more hilarious when Colbert asked his lawyer on the show, "So what's the difference between this and money laundering?"

Potter could only muster, "It's hard to say."

It is nothing new for comics and critics to decry the fact that money is equivalent to power or complain that financial fat cats wield the almighty buck to unjustly influence policy.   By means of this drawn out acted parable, however, Colbert showed the world exactly how corruption happens. Corporations are "people," money is "free speech," and PACs,

Super PACS, and shell corporations allow cash money to compete with the will of the people in politics and policy.

Colbert explained the motivation of his prophetic action satirically to fans and news cameras gathered in front of the FEC buildings in Washington, DC. He declared he his aim was to draw attention to "the American dream. And that dream is simple. That anyone, no matter who they are, if they are determined, if they are willing to work hard enough, someday they could grow up to create a legal entity which could then receive unlimited corporate funds, which could be used to influence our elections."[10]

PROPHET

Stephen Colbert is a prophet. No way? Yahweh![11]

It may well be that his move to the more respectable CBS Network in 2015 might be akin to Jonah who ran and set sail to hide from God and his calling.[12] But I doubt it. It's not that Colbert understands himself as a prophet. I'm quite certain he doesn't. Really, that is probably for the best. But he is one. Stephen Colbert is a prophet.

People have lots of misconceptions about prophets. For one, you might assume that the vocation of prophet involves some

---

[10] Colbert speaking to crowds assembled outside the Federal Elections Commission building on May 13, 2011

[11] "Yahweh or No Way" is a recurring segment on *The Colbert Report* that first launched on January 8, 2009.

[12] In April 2015, CBS announced that Stephen Colbert would take over for David Letterman on *The Late Show* in 2015.

level of moral achievement. In other words, prophets are "good people" or "people of God." Not necessarily.

Again, take Jonah. Jonah tried to abandon his call and flee from God. Why? Because he was suspicious of God's mercy.

In the latter part of the book of Jonah, the prophet becomes "angry enough to die" precisely on account of God's mercy and forgiveness.[13] Jonah illustrates that being a "good guy" is less important than vocation. Jonah was a prophet, commissioned with a message from God to deliver to a particular audience.

Another misconception is that prophets unveil the mysteries of the future. This certainly occurs in the biblical narrative, but prophets are at their best when they shine the light of truth on the present. In other words (as good Bible teachers point out often) prophets are more about "forth-telling" than they are about "fore-telling."

The prophet fearlessly declares that the Emperor has no clothes. He or she elucidates the world right before our eyes that we can't see without outside help. Again, the Chinese parable fits: It's hard to describe water to fish. That is the function of the prophet.

The prophetic vocation is to uncover unseemly and unnoticed realities in ordinary life. For example, hypocrisy and image management we have passively accepted as normative in politics. Or the ideologically and commercially driven narratives we astonishingly accommodate as "objective news

---

[13] Jonah 4:1-5

coverage." Or the narrative that human lives in our nation have a greater value than lives elsewhere in the world. Exposing these lies and laying bare our hypocrisy is the function of the prophetic.

In this way, biblical prophets, the Fake News, and Stephen Colbert are equivalent.

The biblical prophets went to the places of power and told the truth. Usually to kings. Usually involving similar themes: "You've been unfaithful to the God who loves you. You've neglected the plight of the poor, the widow, the orphan, and the alien. You've failed to champion the cause of the voiceless and disenfranchised."

More recently, the voices of Gandhi and Martin Luther King Jr. have been recognized as prophetic. Truth spoken to power regardless of consequences. Similarly, the lived and acted parable of Mother Theresa can be hailed as prophetic.

Those three, of course, are among the greatest human beings of the last hundred years. But there are lessor prophets aplenty.

They are school teachers, social workers, lawyers, Democrats, Republicans, police officers, politicians, homeless, wealthy, and everything in between. Prophets are they who speak the truth, hopefully in love, regardless of the cost.

Even the comic with the courage to speak truth to power.

COURAGE

Stephen Colbert cracks heaps of jokes about "balls."

Colbert frequently presents himself as having the "cojones" to go where angels fear to tread and achieve greatness other pundits would not dare to imagine (except possibly Bill O'Reilly).   The examples he cites to bolster his case of "being ballsy" are almost always ridiculous.

But Stephen Colbert *is* courageous.

The White House Correspondents Dinner in April, 2006 was a momentous comedic event for Stephen Colbert's biggest fans and biggest detractors.   It was arguably the launching point of Colbert's subsequent fame and/or notoriety.[14]

The Colbert Report was a relatively new TV show and naïve president of the White House Press Corps Association Mark Smith invited Stephen Colbert to be the key note speaker. Colbert was not the first comic to be given this honor.   In the past funny men had filled the role, remaining amicable to everyone in attendance while lightly ribbing "the most powerful man in the free world" about character peculiarities or eccentricities.   This time was different.

For twenty seven minutes Stephen Colbert satirized not just the president, but also the news media.   The failures of Washington and the press (particularly with respect to paving the way for war in Iraq) were exposed in poignant, hard hitting

---

[14] Transcript of 2006 Whitehouse Correspondents Dinner speech, Pp. 218-227 *I Am America (And So Can You)* by Stephen Colbert.   New York: Grand Central Publishing (2007).

mock celebration.   The audience of 2,700 (mostly press, politicians, and persons of importance) did not laugh.

No one laughed.   But Colbert did not stop.

The next day, most of the press coverage of Colbert's speech consisted of debating it as "funny" or "not funny."   Opinions and analysis were quite varied.   Nevertheless, the speech was a game changer.   People who had never heard of Stephen Colbert were suddenly paying attention to this comic and *The Colbert Report*.   That same year Colbert was named among Time Magazine's 100 most influential people.[15]

Stephen Colbert was asked if he was making a political statement or if it was "just for laughs."   "Just for laughs," said Colbert.[16]   As in, I was "just" telling the truth.

CREDIBILITY

Some time ago I watched Seattle singer / songwriter David Bazan interviewed by Christian author and thinker David Dark.[17]   The interview was conducted on a theater stage in front of a live audience who were quiet and attentive.

Bazan was getting some backlash in the Christian Evangelical world for his album, *Curse Your Branches,* described by some as a

---

[15] Time 100 online URL:
http://content.time.com/time/specials/packages/article/0,28804,19758
13_1975838_1976306,00.html
[16] In response to *Editor and Publisher*, article reprinted April 22, 2007 URL:
http://www.editorandpublisher.com/Article/FLASHBACK-Stephen-Colb
ert-s-Controversial-Routine-at-Last-Year-s-WHCA-Dinner
[17] "Unsettled Questions" by David Bazan and David Dark on QIdeas.org
Talks.   URL: http://qideas.org/videos/unsettled-questions/

"break up letter" to God. The album dealt with doubt and dissonance, wrestling with God and the Christian narrative. In the interview with Dark, however, Bazan did not appear completely backslidden. While he did reference "smoking weed" (must be a fan of *The Daily Show*) he also seemed comfortable with phrases like "biblical imagination."

The attention grabbing moment of the interview came near the end. David Dark commented, "Poetry is the news that stays news. The classic is 'that which never stops saying what it has to say,' and the idea of the prophetic... Somebody asked Allen Ginsberg, 'How do you become a prophet?' and he said, 'Tell your secrets' it's just as simple as that..."

Precisely at this point Bazan's eyes lit up and he interjected. "You give up so much by doing that! You give up credibility with people but..."

Turning now to the audience he urged them, exhorted them. The man wrestling with whether or not he wanted to be a Christian suddenly became a preacher and declared, "Give up credibility today! Because [that's] the way forward."

"You're not credible. You're full of contradictions. [That's] the only way forward because [credibility] is power. We're all trying to get power over other people and that's all your credibility is - it's when you say something you want people to listen..."

"Credibility is you trying to have power over other people and if you believe in what Jesus said... Which I almost do... You can't be trying to collect power over other people. It's not what he was trying to have you do."

How do you become a prophet? Tell your secrets. Give up credibility today.

In December, 2006 Stephen Colbert was interviewed on Charlie Rose. Charlie asked him about the courage and moxie it must have taken to put himself "out there" like he did in the White House Correspondents Dinner speech. How could he make himself vulnerable to critics, haters, and frankly, risk all his credibility?

Colbert smiled.

Rose had stumbled across the secret of the prophet. He replied grinning: "I have no respectability to protect."[18]

Luke 7:24-26, "What did you go out into the wilderness to see? A reed swayed by the wind? If not, what did you go out to see? A man dressed in fine clothes? No, those who wear expensive clothes and indulge in luxury are in palaces. But what did you go out to see? A prophet? Yes, I tell you, and more than a prophet..."[19]

A comic!

---

[18] "A Conversation With Stephen Colbert" on *Charlie Rose*, aired Dec 8, 2006. Posted by YouTube user "colbertbiter" URL: https://www.youtube.com/watch?v=aDdqd8DdrYM

[19] Luke 7:24-26 *The Holy Bible: New Revised Standard Version.* (1989). Nashville: Thomas Nelson Publishers.

5.

The Funny Pages of Scripture

"Frustration is better than laughter, because a sad face is good for the heart."

Ecclesiastes 7:3[1]

FUNNY

The Bible is not terribly funny. Humor is not altogether absent, but as a general rule, Scripture is not a side-splitter. This raises an important question. If the purest function of comedy is to tell the truth, and the Bible is very concerned with truth, why is this vast and diverse collection of literary forms that we call Sacred Scripture so short on laughs?

On the one hand, 21st century people in an entertainment culture are accustomed to a certain kind of humor. Our sense of humor may not have evolved but it has certainly changed.

---

[1] Ecclesiastes 7:3 *The New International Version*. (2011). Grand Rapids, MI: Zondervan

When humor does show up in the Bible it's usually not the kind we are used to.

On the other hand, it's helpful to note that comedy itself is not always funny.

In the fourteenth century, when Dante penned *The Divine Comedy* he had two categories to choose from; tragedy and comedy. Tragedy was understood as sophisticated literature which involved a bad end for the protagonist. Comedy was considered low art, often written in the vernacular, featuring the protagonist ending up in better circumstances than he or she began.

According to this framework, Scripture contains a great many tragedies, but the Bible as a whole is a comedy.

Genesis launches the comedy by casting humanity mired in sin, rebellion, and death – in need of a God-initiated rescue. The book of Revelation ends with that rescue complete – a restored humanity caught up in the person of Jesus entering the bright and tearless morn characterized by loving and enjoying God forever.

Not funny "ha ha," but in old-school theatrical terms; pure comedy.

We still use the word "comedy" to denote plenty of unfunny stuff. If someone calls an organization a "total comedy," they aren't talking about deep joy or garrulous laughter. When someone says the government is a "joke," they do not mean that politicians are witty or winsome.

In a similar way, satire and parody belong under the umbrella of comedy, but that doesn't make them funny. Satire and parody are usually defined as subsets of comedy.   One could say that satire is a form of comedy and parody is a form of satire but then Stephen Colbert had to muck it up by claiming that "I'm a Satirist...   Satire is parody with a point."[2]

Mockery, lampooning, sarcasm are all part of satire and parody.   They can be engaged hilariously.   On the other hand, they can be used to deliver some biting hurt absent of laughter.   Just ask a person subjected to ridicule or imitation.

It is this sort of unfunny comedy that is plentiful in Scripture. Satire, parody, and sarcasm are frequently employed in ways that leave the "audience" feeling worse instead of better. Nevertheless, while it can have a bitter taste at times, Scripture as a whole is not sour.   The biblical narrative could be described as a grand reverse parody at the center of which is the vindication of fools and foolishness culminating in joy and laughter.   Funny or not.

HUMOR IN THE NEW TESTAMENT

Jesus was a master of hyperbole and comical images.   I've already alluded to the well-known example where Jesus likened Pharisees to people who try to remove a speck from the eye of their brother without noticing the log in their own eye.[3]

Jesus conjured up images of camels passing through the eyes of needles, dead people burying themselves, and old women

---

[2] On *Meet the Press* with David Gregory on NBC, published October 14, 2012.   URL:
http://www.nbcnews.com/video/meet-the-press/49407301
[3] Matthew 7:3-5

throwing parties because they found some loose change while sweeping the floor.[4]

Throughout the gospel narratives, Jesus engages in clever and playful banter with a variety of interlocutors, gives nicknames to disciples, expertly uses hints and indirect communication, tells stories with surprise endings, and responds to questioners by turning assumptions on their head.

In the Temple, enemies who had it out for Jesus asked him whether it was lawful to pay taxes to Caesar.   They were trying to trap him.   A "yes" might be perceived as anti-Jewish-independence and less-than-zealous for God's Kingdom. Meanwhile, a "no" would make him a confessed rebel and guilty of insurrection.

Jesus responded by calling for someone to produce the coin used for paying taxes.   He asked them whose image was on the coin.   "Caesar's," they responded.   Jesus famously declared, "Render unto Caesar what is Caesar's and to God what is God's."[5]

The punch line was brilliant.   His opponents were confounded and amazed.   Quick witted, smart, truthful, and funny.

In Luke's gospel, Jesus appears to two disciples walking down the road to Emmaus on the Sunday of his resurrection.   The couple is downcast and Jesus goes unrecognized as he chats them up about Holy Scripture and his place in the text.   When they arrive at their destination and ask him in for dinner Jesus play acts as if he is going further up the road.   Finally he consents to join them for a meal and "their eyes were opened"

---

[4] Mark 10:25; Luke 9:60; Luke 15:8-10
[5] Matthew 22:21

at the moment he broke bread.[6]   Very subtle, but it certainly has a comic element – especially the bit where Jesus play acted.

Luke uses humor as a literary device more obviously in his second book, The Acts of the Apostles.   Acts tells the story of the early Christian Church after the Ascension of Jesus. When the narrative gets intense, Luke lightens the mood with comedic stories that provide relief.

The first time was when Peter was arrested in Jerusalem.   Late at night, the believers were gathered to pray for the incarcerated Peter.   Lo and behold, an angel released him from prison and he showed up at the prayer meeting, knocking on the door.   A woman named Rhoda came to the door but, seeing Peter, she was so shocked she ran back to the others and forgot to open the door.   Peter was left outside knocking. "Hello?   Anyone?"[7]

That's at least a little funny.   Maybe even the first ever knock-knock joke.

A second instance was in Ephesus.   The Apostle Paul was preaching around town and getting a reputation as a miracle worker.   Seven brothers, the "sons of Sceva," decided they wanted in on his fame and celebrity.   They entered the house of a possessed man and declared to his demons, "In the name of Jesus, who Paul preaches, come out!"   The demon essentially retorted, "I know Jesus and I know Paul, but who the heck are you?"   The seven sons received a world class beat down and ran out of the house... naked![8]

---

[6] Luke 24:13-35
[7] Acts 12:5-16
[8] Acts 19:11-16

Maybe you had to be there.   Like, in the first century.

Later in Acts, Paul was at Troas in a church meeting.   He preached, preached, and preached late into the night.   The sermon was just too much for Eutychus whose name literally means "Lucky" and he fell asleep.   Unlucky for him, he was seated in the sill of a second story window.   He snoozed himself right out the window and fell to the ground below.   Ultimately, the unlucky Lucky caught a lucky break as Paul ran down and declared him A-Okay.[9]

This scene strikes me as funny. Possibly because I've preached sermons and witnessed people falling asleep.   Luckily, I've never preached someone out of a second story window.

CUSSWORDS AND CURSES

In Paul's letters (which comprise most of the New Testament outside of the Gospels and Acts) there are also a few instances that might be called comical.   In Philippians 3:8 Paul used a word that most scholars would agree is a straight up Greek cussword.   He argued that compared with intimately knowing Christ, everything else is σκυβαλα or "scubala."

The word gets translated into English as "refuse," "rubbish," or "dung" but I bet you can imagine a more accurate word – the sort of word a school kid might not say in earshot of their mother.   For most school kids, cusswords can be good for a few giggles.   Maybe for Paul's audience it was the same.

---

[9] Acts 20:7-12

A more biting example of Paul's humor is found in his letter to
the Galatians.   Paul was worked up that some "agitators" were
insisting on circumcision as a requirement for full status
participation in the church.   Paul snidely suggested that since
they seem so fond of knives and circumcision they should put
their knives to good use, go the whole way, and castrate
themselves.   Galatians 5:12.

MORE ON CIRCUMCISION

The Old Testament has a lot more of that biting, dark comedy.
Also on the topic of circumcision, Exodus 34 relates the story
of a head of a guy named Shechem who raped and defiled the
sister of the sons of Jacob.   Not surprisingly, Jacob's sons
boiled with vengeful wrath and started preparing for war
against Shechem and his people.   Instead of engaging the
fight, Shechem tried to "make nice."

Shechem asked for the hand of the young woman in marriage
and proposed a treaty for peace and prosperity between the
men of his city and Jacob's sons.   Jacob's sons seized a golden
opportunity.   Acting as if all was forgiven they responded,
"We'd love to have peace with you, but we can't have dealings
with anyone who is not circumcised so all the adult males of
the city need to be circumcised."

That's not even the punchline.

Remarkably, all the men of the city agreed to be circumcised.
Three days later while they were waylaid and unable to stand
up on account of their sore and healing penises, the sons of

Jacob came in with swords, killed them all, and plundered their town.   Funny or Die?   Apparently both!

One more circumcision story.   In Exodus 4, God told Moses to go to Egypt.   In a strange twist, God met Moses on the road to Egypt intending to slay him dead.   Moses' wife Zipporah quickly jumped into action.   She circumcised their son and put the foreskin on Moses' foot declaring, "I am a bridegroom of blood" and the LORD relented from killing Moses.

Huh?

I don't think that story was intended to be funny.   But, like anything involving feet, it is.

ELIJAH AND THE ALTAR

Elijah facing off against the prophets of Ba'al is a story involving intentional and grim humor.   God's prophet Elijah was deeply offended by idol worship in the land of Israel.   To combat it, he invited 450 prophets of the Philistine deity Ba'al to a contest against the God of Israel.

Two altars for sacrifice were set up – one for Ba'al and one for Israel's God.   The rules of the game were that each of the religious rivals would take turns calling down fire from heaven upon their offerings.

The prophets of Ba'al went first.   Dancing in a frenzy they called on their god for fire.

Elijah was not merely a comic, he was a heckler. He mocked and taunted them. They danced harder. Then Elijah really started baiting them, "Maybe your god is sleeping? Maybe he's on a journey? Shout a little louder and perhaps he'll get out of bed and come to your aid."

Nada.

Finally it was Elijah's turn. First, he had the altar to Israel's God soaked in water repeatedly for dramatic effect. Then, with a simple prayer, fire fell from God in heaven consuming everything. The not-so-nice part is that the 450 prophets of Ba'al were taken into a valley and slaughtered.[10]

In a scene like this, parody is blatantly operative but "funny" is not the right word.

IDOLS

As in the story above, Scripture regularly employs parody in polemics against idolatry. In the whole Bible from beginning to end, idolatry is far and away Enemy of God Numero Uno.

Unfortunately, many people assume that the Bible is mostly about God telling people what not to do. Part of this, no doubt, stems from the grammatical construction of the Ten Commandments which exhort, "Thou Shalt Not..."

I would argue that the Bible is ultimately about "freedom to" and not "constraint from." Nevertheless, if you wanted to identify the "sin" that is most often and most passionately

---

[10] 1 Kings 18:16-40

condemned in Scripture it is idolatry – worshiping created things in place of the Creator.

It bears mentioning that the second most condemned infraction (and linked to idolatry) is a failure to take care of the poor and disenfranchised. But while neglect for the poor is responded to with wrath, incredulity, and sadness in Scripture, idolatry is attacked viciously with both satire and mockery. The Scriptures cast those who put faith in wealth, power, nation states, false gods, or anything temporal in place of God as ridiculous and worthy of ridicule.

The prophet Isaiah even does something like a stand-up routine along these lines:

"Get a load of this… A guy goes outside and cuts down a tree. He drags it home. He chops half of it up to cook his food and warm his house. The other half he carves a face, some eyes, a nose, and a body. Then he bows down and says, "You're my god! Save me and bring me good fortune!" Can you believe that? Dummies! They're just like their gods – eyes that don't see, ears that don't hear. They're worshiping a block of wood for Goodness' sake!"

This is my paraphrase of Isaiah 44 as observational comedy. It might not "kill" at the comedy club but its function is to expose the ridiculous and illuminate truth.

Again, truth is best apprehended in slanted speech – even "fake" speech.

SARCASM

The extreme of fake speech is sarcasm – saying the opposite of what you mean to get a point across.   In Scripture, one of the best instances of sarcasm is espoused by God himself.   While not concerning idolatry directly, the book of Job is structured like a play.   The stage is set with a wager between God and the devil but then features several voices weighing in on questions about why there is evil and suffering; why good people seem to suffer while the wicked prosper.

For the first part of the dialogue, God is silent.   Finally, after being questioned and challenged by Job God speaks up and engages in first class sarcasm.   It went something like this:

"Oh... I'm sorry Job. You're right. I remember now. You were there when I called creation into being out of nothing with a word of my mouth. Right, it must have slipped my mind that when I was setting mountains and seas and stars and worlds in their places that you, Job, were there with me. Or when I appointed the times and dates for the world and breathed life into beings and gave them life... I remember, it was you old buddy, old pal, Job who was there with me."[11]

REVERSE PARODY

Scripture acknowledges and utilizes satire, parody, sarcasm, and mockery to illuminate truth.   Better than going for laughs, it holds up a mirror to our world that can't be accomplished with straight speech.

---

[11] Job 38-41

This paradox of comedy – whether in Fake News or Scripture – is a marvel.

How is it that it takes such a high level of abstraction in order to effectively communicate truth? How is it that espousing the opposite of truth can illuminate truth better than a simple explanation?

Here again is the sinful human condition. Comedy is not the problem but the nature of the problem is such that few things can address it as well as comedy. Human pride, one-upsmanship, selfishness, money-worship, power-worship, and all the other garbage that constitutes the "real" world where we live, breathe, and work are, in fact, a parody of God's creation. To criticize the parody, few mechanisms are more effective than parody itself.

One of the most disturbing and yet prevailing spiritual teachings of the entire Bible is that you become like what you worship.

If you worship money, you will become a consumer who sees everything including people as commodities to be used. If you worship power, you will become compassionless and incapable of love. If you worship sex, you will exchange a reverence of human personhood in favor of using people for selfish ends.

Bob Dylan said as much in his 1974 hit "You Gotta Serve Somebody" but the Bible said it first.

In Psalm 115, the psalmist begins with a comedy routine almost identical to Isaiah's. Idols, he argues, are a creepy parody of God and humanity made in his image. They have mouths but can't speak, eyes but can't see, ears but can't hear, noses that can't smell, hands that can't touch, feet that can't walk – they can't even clear their throats or utter a sound.

The parody is concluded with a dark prophesy in the Psalm's eighth verse, "Those who make them will end up just like them, so will all who trust in them."

Jesus used exactly this imagery explaining to his disciples why the religious leaders rejected him. "They are ever looking but never perceiving, ever hearing but not understanding…" In short, they were idolatrous and had become deaf, dumb, and blind like the idols they worshiped. The worst thing about the Pharisees was that their idolatry was conducted in the name of God.

This reverse parody is at the heart of the Christian narrative. The whole world which follows its own way becomes a parody of God's creation. The systems we create and participate in, our structures of authority, our politics, our economics, our religious sensibilities, our social formulas – all are parodies.

"Friend of the show" (i.e. one time guest on *The Colbert Report*) and New Testament scholar N.T. Wright has described the gospel according to Paul in terms of the uncovering of a colossal parody. In the shadow of the greatest empire the world had ever known (Rome), Wright argues, to declare Jesus as "Lord" is to say that Jesus is the reality of which Caesar the Emperor is the parody.[12]

This audacious perspective is crucial for understanding Paul – arguably the New Testament's greatest thinker.

---

[12] An argument made repeatedly across numerous lectures, papers, and books by N.T. Wright. See also URL: http://ntwrightpage.com/

In the century that Jesus died, Rome had achieved dominion over all – economic prosperity, world peace based on military might, and splendor without rival.   Caesar was hailed across the Mediterranean world as both savior and lord – the undisputed heavy weight champion of the world.

For anyone who demurred, the sign of Rome's dominance was crucifixion.   Only a few miles from Nazareth when Jesus was probably about ten years old, two thousand people were crucified in one day for opposing Rome.   There was no question who reigned and who was lord.

Except for people like Paul.

Paul even had the audacity to say of Jesus; "Having disarmed the powers and authorities, he made a public spectacle of them, triumphing over them by the cross."[13]

This statement is ridiculous.   Crosses existed to make a public spectacle of insurrectionists, not the other way around. Nevertheless, Paul firmly maintained faith in a future vindication of sufferers.   He believed this was guaranteed by the resurrection of Jesus.

In Paul's own story, it is precisely this faith that allowed him to confidently face and endure imprisonments, beatings, stonings, false accusations, and ultimately execution at the hands of the same Empire the cross had emptied of its power.

Paul, however, did not invent the idea that Jesus is the reality of which Caesar was only a parody.   It is rooted in the gospels themselves.

---

[13] Colossians 2:15

All four accounts of Jesus earthly life develop the plot line involving the disciples (and many besides) carrying a mounting expectation that Jesus ministry would culminate in a triumphant takeover and a coronation of Jesus as King in Jerusalem for Judea if not the world.

This expectation is contrasted with Jesus knowingly taking the way of sorrow and submitting, eventually, to death itself.

The passion-filled and somewhat tragic subtext of story the gospels tell is that the disciples had bought into the parody version of reality – the version of reality we might describe as "our normal way of looking at the world" that affirms a "might is right" kind of power.   Jesus, meanwhile, reveals what God is like against our parodies and even against the ways we have type-casted God himself – distant, condemning, violent, etc. Against these, Jesus chose the lonely and misunderstood way of self-giving love – the way of the cross.

The trial, mocking, and crucifixion of Jesus in this way are the most poignant revelation of God in Scripture while steeped in the deepest possible irony.   Shortly after Roman governor Pilate (a puppet of the parody) and Jesus (the reality) banter about the meaning of power, kingship, and truth; Jesus was dressed in purple, given a crown of thorns, mocked as royalty, and executed as a failed rebel under a sign reading "King of the Jews."[14]

The irony, of course, is that the disciples were right.   Jesus ministry indeed culminated with his coronation in Jerusalem as King of Kings.   His murder was his coronation.   His very

---

[14] John 18:28-19:22

subjection to mockery, defeat, and death exposed the parody of earthly powers.   Appearances can be deceiving.

In 1 Corinthians Paul calls the cross "foolishness" to those who value wisdom, but counters that the "foolishness of God" trumps humanity's loftiest wisdom.[15]   A couple of chapters later he advocates being "fools for Christ" who have been crucified to the values of the world and reborn in love and the Spirit.[16]

Strength in weakness, victory in death.

This grand reversal becomes the story of all of Scripture to be sounded yet again at its conclusion in the Book of Revelation. In the apocalyptic vision of John the Revelator, John is weeping and weeping because no one has been found worthy to break the seals and open the scrolls.

Finally, his sorrow is lifted when he hears that the Lion of the Tribe of Judah is worthy to accomplish what needs doing.   He turns to look at this ferocious king of beasts and he sees what looks like a lamb slain.[17]   As my old Bible teacher put it, "The only lion in heaven is a slain lamb."[18]

Caesar's lordship, "might is right," and the worship of power are laid bare and exposed as parody by the narrative of Scripture.   That's the joke the Bible tells.   Its exposé is accomplished through hyperbole, wit, satire, sarcasm and parody against parody.   Ultimately, though, the bankruptcy of our godless parody is exposed by the scandal if not the comedy

---

[15] 1 Corinthians 1:14-25
[16] 1 Corinthians 3:18-19, 4:10
[17] Revelation 5:1-10
[18] Gordon Fee, as remembered by the author.

of the cross itself – the cross that vindicates fools courageous enough to believe it as surely as it vindicates the Divine Fool himself.

6.

Parrhesia

"There is no fear in love.   Perfect love casts out fear, because fear
has to do with consequences"

1 John 4:18[1]

JOKER IS WILD

In a standard deck of playing cards, Kings, Queens, and Jacks
are stately and stern.   The Jack of Diamonds, nicknamed the
Laughing Jack, is sometimes smirking.   The King of Hearts
has no mustache and some call him the Suicide King on
account of how he holds his sword.   The Queen of Hearts has
on occasion been identified as the Jewish heroine Judith.   But
only the Joker is wild.

Donning a floppy, three-pointed hat with jingle balls and
sporting a devilish grin – the Joker stands out among the cards.

---

[1] 1 John 4:18, author's translation

He is the fool, the mocker, the clown, the buffoon.   Loyal to no particular suit he transcends them all.

The character of the Joker on playing cards, of course, is intended to be analogous to the jester from old Europe's royal courts.   In medieval times, jesters weren't just leftovers in the deck – they occupied a vital role and function in the kingdom. More than merely fools, they were fools who told the truth.

Kings wielded ultimate power and authority, even the power of life and death over their subjects.   It was in everyone's best interest to please the king and remain in his good graces.   The inevitable side effect was that a king would be surrounded by "Yes Men" – people conditioned to respond to every royal decree, idea, or notion with enthusiastic approval. Unfortunately, the actual merit of the king's policies and positions might become secondary.

Running a kingdom (I'm told) takes wisdom, cunning, and deep thinking about serious matters from every possible angle. Kings needed advisors to guide and help them lead, but they also needed people willing to be brutally honest with him.   But who would dare to be so honest?   Honest enough to risk losing their head for the sake of truth?

Enter the court jester.

The jester was a fool, but a fool with a function.   He might well be assailed as a madman and an idiot.   But as a fool he was also exempt from punishment and given freedom to mock, criticize, and scoff at any and all happenings in the kingdom.

Only the Fool, without repercussion, could point out how the Duke was using his daughter as sexual leverage to secure a parcel of land.

Only the Idiot could mockingly suggest that the Queen's cold attitude stemmed from growing resentment and collusion with the king's rival.

Only the Jester could laughingly assert that the flattery of the Treasurer had more to do with the Treasurer's lavish lifestyle than the greatness of the king.

Only the Buffoon could lampoon the king over his foolhardy, ego driven plan to invade that neighboring country which would almost certainly result in his ruin.

The role of everyone else in the kingdom involved perpetuating a public façade – the king's greatness, his divine right to rule. The role of the Jester was to expose it. He was the only one who could speak truth with no consequences.

More than a fool's errand, truth telling was the jester's mandate.

The Joker was often hated or considered dangerous by other members of the court for relentlessly exposing their motives and weaknesses. Though he would skewer the king more thoroughly than the rest, the wise king would protect the Fool as the only one with the guts to do it. He was the conscience of the empire, a comic reminder to pay attention to sanity behind the insanity of political angling, one-upsmanship, pride, pomp, and posturing.

NO CONSEQUENCES

For comedy to function properly it has to operate freely and without consequences. Accountability and responsibility don't just drain the laughter out of comedy, they rob its ability to tell the truth. For comedy to operate as a spotlight on reality, an almost reckless permissiveness is required.

If you are familiar with just how raw and offensive some comedians can be, this may seem like a strange claim. I'm not saying that we should find any manner of distasteful joke funny or truthful, merely that diminishing the range of comedy through censorship is directly proportional to its ability to hit the target of truth.

You can use words to build up or tear down. If you're skilled, you can even use words that build up to tear down and words that tear down to build up. I'm not arguing that rude comics should not be declared rude. Not everyone should be given a microphone.

To the extent you limit the freedom of any voice, you limit that voice's ability to tell the truth.

If sex jokes are forbidden, speaking the truth about sexuality is also forbidden. In certain contexts, this limitation may well be appropriate. At the same time, it is hearing the truth about human sexuality that makes sex jokes funny. Sex jokes aren't funny unless they make us confront something true – our views, taboos, assumptions, or fears concerning sex. The very experience of being shocked or offended is often just a forced confrontation with our real selves and our real ideas. This does not justify the one who delivers the shock and offense – it's simply an observation.

Limitations, restrictions, and boundaries limit the field of truth telling. In doing so, they necessarily limit the risk of the "hearer" confronting truth.

In dictatorial regimes, this is the aim of censorship. Censorship is designed to remove the possibility of media undermining assumptions and ideologies. When comedy is censored the principle is the same. Limiting the range of comedy puts "kid gloves" on it and strips it of its authentic power.

Of course, playing Chris Rock or Luis CK at your ten year old daughter's princess party is a bad idea. That would be foolishness (and not in a good way). While limitations might sometimes be appropriate the principal remains intact; consequences kill comedy.

The suppression of truth by fear of pain or punishment is exactly the logic that was behind giving license to jesters. If you have to choose your words too carefully, choosing no words at all will always be safest. On the other hand, if a comic is given unrestricted leeway to say whatever they want, what comes out just might be the truth.

What remains is the glorious vocation of the comic. A job with no consequences, no responsibility, and no accountability. Nevertheless, it is far from easy. It demands you tell the truth. A dangerous calling.

FIRST AMENDMENT

The most obvious mechanism for protecting the voice of the comic against consequences in America is Freedom of Speech. Just as kings granted the court fools license to lampoon, the First Amendment of the Constitution theoretically grants fools of every sort the right say any blessed thing they want.

Freedom of speech became law in 1791 to protect against suppression and oppression by political overlords. The Amendment insists on a free press whereby people can criticize, question, and explore any manner of thing openly without fear of Gulag or guillotine. It acknowledges that privileging or suppressing voices violates freedom and undermines democracy.

Freedom of speech, of course, also has unintended consequences. Opening the door of dialogue to all people equally involves opening it to idiots. There is no shortage of stupid, hateful, untrue, and derisive ideas which have been spread thanks to the right of free speech. Nevertheless, it is generally agreed that the freedom is worth the cost.

If certain voices are going to be privileged over others, the one who decides which voices get privileged is guilty of tyranny. While I hail Stephen Colbert as a prophet there are at least as many who would count him as an idiot (which I suppose he also is). For freedom of speech to function it has to be given to all.

Unfortunately, the ideal of free speech and equal opportunity is not always completely realized in America (like the concepts of "democracy," or "politicians who are public servants"). If I have a megaphone and you do not, my speech is privileged. And if I have a nationally broadcast television program?

But television is not the only way to privilege voices and skew freedom of speech. Stephen Colbert regularly (and gleefully) points out that we live in an America where corporations are people and money equals free speech. The inescapable result is that more money means more free speech.

This is hard to overestimate in an age where corporate wealth and power have seized control of the volume knob of public discourse. The invisible hand of the market has an invisible voice. Any loud or effective voice in our culture should be suspected of having corporate interests behind it.

Statements by politicians, anchors, and entertainers should be weighed on their merit... But also in light of their sponsorship.

This is one of the biggest critiques of so-called "objective" news media outlets. It is more than legitimate to question the extent to which corporate interests determine not only how stories get covered, but what is considered "newsworthy" in the first place. For 24-hour news channels, saving corporate dollars has involved removing correspondents from worldwide locations, filling time instead with "cheaper" panels of arguing analysts, and even delving into product placement or "covering" the news story of a recently released piece of technology by a major brand.

Long gone, it seems, is the old journalistic ideal of uncovering truth to serve and empower the interests of the public. This ideal is laughable. So laughable that shows like *The Daily Show* and *The Colbert Report* exist.

But what about the comedians themselves? Who are *their* sponsors? Do the kings who protect jesters like Stephen Colbert and Jon Stewart pursue the best interest of the public? Or are the voices of the comic critics co-opted by the establishment they oppose (like the entrepreneur who makes money hand over fist selling "Down with Capitalism" T-shirts)?

Suspicion is always warranted. But for Colbert and Stewart I would suggest the situation is far less cynical.

STANDARDS

On the one hand, the Fake News cannot be judged according the same standard as the "real" news. The "real" news operates on the premise of objectivity, the Fake News does not. The "real" news promises to deliver content for the sake of the public interest, the Fake News makes no such claim.

Jon Stewart has drawn criticism, for example, of being too "soft" on political interviewees and accused that *The Daily Show* hypocritically embodies the same biases or lack of meaningful content for which he skewers the "real" news. If this were a valid critique, however, it would be paramount to an admission that the "real" news itself has become a parody of itself.

When comedy and parody are judged on the same basis or by the same criteria, credibility has gone out the window.

Jon Stewart attempted to point this out in an interview on *Fox News Sunday* with Chris Wallace.

"Here is the difference between you and I," Stewart argued. "I'm a comedian first. My comedy is informed by an ideological background. There's no question about that... [But] I'm not an activist. I'm a comedian... Do I want my voice heard? Absolutely. That's why I got into comedy."[2]

Jesters are jesters. They do not function in the same way or play by the same rules as journalists or politicians. It is not "offside" for Stephen Colbert to sip a Bud Light Lime or crunch on tasty Doritos during a broadcast and get paid for it. For Colbert, in fact, it is part of drawing attention to sponsorship for his audience causing them to question which snack and beer companies might be behind the other sources of information they trust and depend on.

This is not to say comics are beyond scrutiny. "No consequences" does not mean there can be no complaints or counter arguments. It would be naïve to ignore the dollars behind comedic platforms and or not question whose cash is funding whose comedy. In the case of Stephen Colbert and Jon Stewart, however, there are few secret or sinister machinations.

WHOSE NETWORK IS IT ANYWAY?

The parent company of Comedy Central is Viacom, the Sumner Redstone controlled telecommunications giant. More technically, Viacom is the parent of MTV Networks

---

[2] *Fox News Sunday With Chris Wallace* interview with Jon Stewart, June 19, 2011. Transcript and video of entire episode at URL: http://www.foxnews.com/on-air/fox-news-sunday/transcript/defense-s ecretary-robert-gates-exit-interview-jon-stewart-talks-politics-media-bi as#p//v/1007141824001

which is the parent of Comedy Central. Like any network, commercials, products, and therefore corporate interests are its bread and butter. Still, aside from its ability to generate ratings, the "voice" of Stephen Colbert is not heavily scrutinized and perhaps not taken that seriously.

Colbert has always claimed the network gave him enormous freedom to pursue the comedy he wanted.

"They read all the scripts," he said, but insisted that beyond not doing what is illegal, no one ever asked him to change jokes.[3]

"They might say something like, "Please don't say McDonalds gives you cancer,"" Colbert stated, ""But if there was a news story that said McDonalds gives you cancer" they would say go ahead."[4]

Viacom and Redstone even put up with being the butt of more than a few jokes on *The Colbert Report*. Their restraint from censorship or control may not be because of a firm commitment to free speech, but as long as the ratings are high and the sponsors are buying, large and diverse entertainment companies know well enough to let their underlings do their thing in relative peace and freedom.

One of the inherent advantages of comedy (and art in general) is that it is mostly subjective and open to interpretation. As a result, the voice of the comic is more difficult to suppress and control.

---

[3] *The Paul Mecurio Show* (#26) interview with Stephen Colbert on August 12, 2013. Podcast URL: http://sideshownetwork.tv/podcastsEpisode.cfm?podcastid=68&episodeID=2659
[4] Ibid.

Still, it happens.

While Comedy Central has never been terribly discriminating (although the network once pulled the plug on an episode of *South Park* when its creators were set to portray a cartoon image of the Prophet Muhammad),[5] things are different elsewhere in the world.

In Egypt, a heart surgeon named Bassem Yousseff started a humble YouTube series of political critiques modeled after *The Daily Show*. In the wake of the Arab Spring and the fall of President Mubarak, the show rocketed in popularity, became a hit TV program, and gained a Middle Eastern viewership of over 8 million.

Despite its continuing popularity, Youseff ended his show in 2014 citing concerns for his own safety after experiencing lawsuits, a banned episode, and other "pressures" in and outside of Egypt.[6]

Truth telling is dangerous. Comedy raises the stakes. To function properly as critic and revealer of truth, the comedic voice must be protected and given freedom to function without consequences. Democracy may not have achieved a society where people are king, but we must protect our jesters.

---

[5] See other controversies and tussles with Comedy Central in the following Wikipedia article URL:
http://en.wikipedia.org/wiki/South_Park_controversies
[6] See *Bassem Youssef Abruptly Cancels Egyptian Satire Show Before Sisi Declared President* by Jarid Malsin in Time, June 3, 2014. URL: http://time.com/2818306/bassem-youssef-abruptly-cancels-egyptian-satire-show-before-sisi-declared-president/

PARRHESIA

Democracy, as a concept, was dreamt up in Ancient Greece. It meant something different then.

For one, it wasn't the comics who took on the horrible weight of being truth tellers in public forums, it was the philosophers. Instead of "buffoonery," they came up with a respectable word: parrhesia or παρρησια. Translated, it is typically rendered "boldness," "confidence," or better still, "free speech."

The novel idea of the Greeks was that more voices would bring about better ideas. They reasoned that if play-writes and politicians were able to say what they *really* thought, the truth would rise to the top. Wisely, they did not limit the "permission to speak freely" to politicians. It was granted to all Athenians.

Then, as now, an interesting pattern emerged. Artists and comedians were more likely to use their freedom of speech to say what they really believed while politicians were more likely to employ their right to remain silent.

Pandering for laughs is done best when uncovering truth. Pandering for votes, on the other hand, compels politicians to cover up the truth.

In our democracy, politicians exist to represent the populace and serve the common good – to create a better society through representation, passing laws, and forming policies. Just like in Ancient Greece, the old European courts where jesters served, or at pretty much any other time or place in history; this political ideal is and has been regularly compromised by competing interests. Money, power, party pressure, corporate influence, lobbies, nepotism, greed, and pride weigh heavily in most political systems.

If politicians are engineers of society creators and kingdom builders, comics are there to test what they build with fire. Comedy is criticism. Aimed to expose lies, pull apart faulty logic, subvert narratives, question emphases, draw attention to the unspoken, and be an irritant for good – the voice that tells it like it really is, not succumbing to what itchy ears want to hear, and bearing witness to the truth behind the truthiness.

This deeply vocational sense of truth telling is what the Greeks were trying to get at with the concept of parrhesia.

While free speech was granted to Athenian citizens, Greek society suppressed a number of voices. Women, slaves, and foreigners were not granted free speech of any kind. Nevertheless, as a philosophical concept, parrhesia was not simply about ensuring the legal right for underdogs to pipe up on whatever subject they pleased. On the contrary, it was an invitation to an existential state-of-being involving a commitment to complete openness and honesty in the service of truth itself.

BIBLE WORD GAME

Parrhesia was applied to politics by the ancient Greeks. But parrhesia is a robust concept that transcends social, religious, and political categories. I make this claim because parrhesia is also a Bible word. But before digging deeper into that word, let's look at another Bible word. Love.

The function of comedy is to tell the truth. Comedy can only tell the truth effectively if it is unshackled from responsibility, accountability, and the fear of consequences. If all this is so, how do we differentiate the glorious light of truth from dirty jokes for cheap laughs? Comedy is redemptive when the impetus is love.

In his letter to the Ephesians the Apostle Paul suggested restraint when it came to dirty jokes, but a chapter earlier he exhorted the church against duplicity by "speaking the truth in love" and thereby growing to maturity together in the One who is truth's Author.[7]

Ever since Paul penned those words, "speaking the truth in love" has become a rule of thumb for wise Jesus-followers to bear in mind. Basically, "Speaking the truth in love" simply means "tell the truth but don't be a jerk about it." I've heard it said that truth without compassion is cruelty.

At a deeper level, the commitment to speak the truth in love is the recognition that the very thing that drives human relationships with each other and with God is a partnership between truth and love.

This partnership also drives comedy. Not in the sense that comedy should be lovey-dovey or romantic, but in the sense that it is driven by a love of truth. Even when comedy is angry it should be driven by a love of truth. Its enemy, meanwhile, is fear. In this way comedy is just like relationships or life itself. While a love of truth, vulnerability, authenticity, and love make all things better, against these stands fear.

---

[7] Ephesians 4:15

Fear is a Bible word, too.   In the narrative of Scripture, fear functions not only as an enemy of laughter but as an enemy of relationship – relationships between humans and relationships between humans and God.   Whenever God or an angel appears to a person in Scripture the response of the person is always to be seized with fear.   The divine answer, meanwhile, is always and again, "Do not be afraid."

"Do not be afraid, I bring you good news of great joy that will be for all people…"

Consider a pair of lovers.   The greatest depth of relationship is when they are able to give themselves completely to the other – physically, emotionally, spiritually.   This level of freedom, intimacy, and authenticity can only be achieved if acceptance and love is total and fear is completely absent.

Fear of what?

The same fear that grips us when we encounter God.   Fear of rejection.   Fear of condemnation.   If you see me as I really am, if you see my innermost being…   You will reject me.   Yet only if I dare to hope against hope and open up my true self – only then can I receive love and experience acceptance.   Truth and love together alone make authenticity possible.   Like the Scripture says, "perfect love casts out fear."

In precisely this sense, truth telling is not only an important but a sacred endeavor.   And this is why comedy must have no consequences.   Fear of consequences excludes authenticity. A guarded heart cannot be true.   Comedy simultaneously breaks down the fear of consequences and enables us to face more truth.

This is a functioning dialectic. Comedy is about telling the truth. You can't tell the truth when you are afraid. When fear is gone and you are able to tell the truth, comedy is better.

As Colbert argued, it is physiologically impossible to laugh and be afraid at the same time. Comedy itself breaks down the fear of consequences completing the circle, pulling us upward to enable more truth and better comedy.

LOVE HURTS?

Comedy wields the sword of truth in all sorts of ways that are loveless and cruel. From snide and sarcastic remarks at the dinner table to public mocking and humiliation, comedy can tell the truth in the service of tearing down as well as building up.

As we saw in Scripture itself, tearing down systems and institutions of evil and oppression is good and necessary. Meanwhile, tearing down your Cousin Bill's self-worth with jokes about his outfit is neither good nor necessary.

But when love is present comedy is elevated to something that builds up. Truth is always costly. Engaging truth is always a risk. The truth can hurt. Love opens up the door for truth to be heard. And comedy aids the whole process. Again according to Stephen Colbert, "Comedy helps an idea go down."[8]

---

[8] On *Meet the Press* with David Gregory on NBC, published October 14, 2012. URL:
http://www.nbcnews.com/video/meet-the-press/49407301

Consider an example of how this functions in daily life. Suppose you are afraid to broach a topic with someone you love.   You are afraid that if you tell the truth or let them know what you *really* think you might damage the relationship, experience rejection, etc.   A common way to "make room" for greater authenticity is to make a joke.   Get at the topic sideways through comedy to "test the waters" and softly open up the space for greater dialogue.

We do not wear our hearts on our sleeves.

We communicate indirectly, almost always resisting open confrontation.   We come at issues sideways not because we don't care enough to address the issue openly and authentically but because too much openness too fast "shuts doors" in the human psyche.

On a larger scale, consider jokes about ethnicity, political leanings, or stereotypes. If we're not offended they can open up space to reconsider how we view ourselves and how we view those who are "other" in order to arrive at greater authenticity.

It's sensitive.   It's dangerous.   It requires love.   But it is by toppling consequences and emptying threats that greater truth can be faced.

PASTOR'S CONFERENCE

The other day I was listening to a podcast featuring a round table discussion of comedian friends.   This cohort of comics were discussing their specific craft.   In this case, stand-up.

The discussion was not at all what I expected. What I heard both moved and amazed me.

As a preacher and speaker I have participated in numerous conversations and collectives discussing the craft of speech – the need to connect with audiences, strategies for communication, the use of story and parable, biblical accuracy, authenticity. Nevertheless, listening to this gaggle of comics I felt nothing short of jealous.

They talked about their vocations with passion – arguing that being a stand-up comedian was more of an identity and destiny then a chosen career path.

They talked about authenticity and telling the truth. They challenged each other to make themselves vulnerable and insisted that excellence required baring open their souls and giving every part of themselves away for the sake of their art and audience.

It struck me that I have rarely heard preachers talk like that, but it sounded a lot like Jesus. What moved me was the self-emptying commitment to truth in genuine love. Again I thought of the words of David Bazan, "Give up credibility today."[9]

You become a prophet by telling your secrets. Conversely, beware of the person who has too much to lose. The truth of their voice might be compromised by fear.

On *Meet the Press* in 2008 Stephen Colbert gave away the secret of his comedy. Tim Russert marveled at how Colbert

---

[9] "Unsettled Questions" by David Bazan and David Dark on QIdeas.org Talks.   URL: http://qideas.org/videos/unsettled-questions/

fearlessly took on big issues like the president and powers that be.   Colbert responded grinning, "Right!   There are no consequences."[10]

ESTHER AND THE KING OF KINGS

The biblical story of Esther involves double crossing, murder, wild tempers, an illicit harem, misogyny, drunkenness, accusations of cheating, near genocide, fear, hatred, unbelievable courage, the abuse of power, risk taking, and lives hanging in the balance.

As such, it is a pretty typical Bible story.

Esther is set in the reign and palace of Xerxes of Persia where the people of Israel were in exile.   Cyrus had granted free passage of Jews back to the Holy Land but many stayed behind including Mordecai and his beautiful step-daughter Esther.

Xerxes wife, Queen Vashti, refused to appear before him at the conclusion of a seven day drinking party.   Vashti was having a party of her own and, evidently, resented being summoned for the entertainment of Xerxes and his guests.

King Xerxes banned her from his presence, stripped her of her power, and, basically, opened up auditions across the kingdom for who would be his next wife.   Esther pleased the king and was crowned queen over all the land.

---

[10] *Meet the Press (TAKE TWO: msnbc.com)* with Tim Russert online exclusive aired October 21, 2007.   URL: http://www.nbcnews.com/video/meet-the-press/21400561#21400561

The story, however, is not merely a tale of rags to riches.   The climax comes when Esther's step-father Mordecai was about to be hung on a gallows by order of royal decree thanks to the scheming of Mordecai's arch enemy Haman - the king's right hand man.   Moreover, the entire Jewish race were being threatened with genocide and the only possible person who might advocate on behalf of Mordecai and the Jews was Esther.

The trouble, though, was that no one was permitted to enter into the presence of the king uninvited.   If they did, they would stand before him condemned to die except, by chance, if the king would extend his scepter as a gesture of grace.

No scepter, no quarter.

Esther was understandably hesitant.   Not only had she kept it a secret from the king that she was a Jew, she had not been summoned by the king in over thirty days.   She once pleased the king but now she did not know where she stood.   Stepping into his presence would be literally putting her life on the line for her people.   Of course, this is exactly what she did.

Mordecai declared, "Perhaps you came to your royal position for such a time as this."   She resolved that she would go before the king "even if I die."   Happily, the scepter was extended and she was granted mercy in his presence.   Fear gave way to acceptance.   Free speech was initiated. Consequences were vanquished.

"Ask anything," declared the king, "Even up to half the kingdom."

Because of her risk which saved the Jews and her willingness to die for her people, Esther is celebrated to this day as a biblical hero.   Every year, her story is re-enacted by Jews in the festival of Purim.   For Christians, she is nothing short of a picture of Christ.

Jesus, too, was "born for such a time as this" as the Gospels point out.   Like Esther, the story of Jesus comes to a climax when he puts his life on the line for the sake of his people.   He was not spared but his people were freed from death and sin. Through his death and triumphing over the grave Scripture says God not only offered Jesus "up to half the kingdom" but put all things under his feet.   Above all, he was granted freedom to approach the throne. Freedom that he extends to all people in his name.

And finally we come full circle.   This freedom has a name. Parrhesia. Parrhesia as an existential and vocational way of being in complete authenticity before God and all creation. Parrhesia which is barren of consequences.

Parrhesia is an interesting word in the Bible.   When Jesus spoke "plainly" (as opposed to in parables) it was parrhesia.[11] When Paul prayed for courage to speak before kings, it was parrhesia.[12]   When something was done publicly for all to see, it was parrhesia.[13]   But most purely and beautifully, when Hebrews and 1 John talk about how we approach the throne of God, they use the word parrhesia.[14]

---

[11] John 16:29

[12] Ephesians 6:19-20

[13] Colossians 2:15

[14] Parrhesia is a word and concept which appears four times in Hebrews and another four times in the short letter of 1 John.

In the passage where John says "perfect love casts out fear" the larger context is love, truth, and parrhesia.   God is love, says John.   We are perfected in love, says John.   There is no fear in love, says John, because fear has to do with fear of punishment and perfect love casts out fear.[15]

In Jesus, says John, there is nothing to fear from the one who says, "Come, all who are thirsty."[16]

Do not be afraid.

In him we have boldness, confidence, permission to speak freely in the speech of lovers.   The speech of those vulnerable. The speech of those accepted.

The gospel, ultimately, is that fools and jesters like you and me are given license to live, laugh, and thrive fearlessly in the throne room of the King.

---

[15] 1 John 4:16-18
[16] Isaiah 55:1; Revelation 22:17

7.

Mocking the Sacred

"Do not be deceived: God cannot be mocked. A man reaps what he sows."

Galatians 6:7[1]

GET SERIOUS

Relevant Magazine posted, "6 Times Stephen Colbert Got Serious About Faith."[2] The online article counted moments when Stephen Colbert's authentic religious beliefs showed through the cracks of his character's façade. The comment section was relatively tame except for a certain David O'Brian who wrote:

---

[1] Galatians 6:7 *The New International Version*. (2011). Grand Rapids, MI: Zondervan.
[2] "6 Times Stephen Colbert Got Serious About Faith" by Jesse Carey, April 14, 2014. Relevant Magazine Online. URL: http://www.relevantmagazine.com/culture/6-times-stephen-colbert-got -serious-about-faith#fm2ckG6kVQ5KsmzM.99

"What a load of crap. This pervert (Colbert) repeatedly blasphemes Jesus (including insinuations that Jesus was a homosexual)... This "magazine" lacks discernment and integrity.   Or maybe it's just as perverted as Colbert."[3]

Not everyone is a fan.

The irate comment raises something worth considering.   For every six times that Stephen Colbert "gets serious about his faith," there are sixty-six times he is consciously and intentionally *unserious* about his faith.   People uncomfortable with Jesus jokes, making sport of doctrines, and roasting Christian culture find Colbert a tough pill to swallow.

Is this the medicine we need?   Or is Colbert merely an opportunist exploiting 2000 years of cultural heritage to garner laughs?

The answer is yes.

2000 years of Christian heritage has also afforded 2000 years of opportunities to get distracted from what really matters. Subjecting religion to the wily whims of irreverent comedians can be a corrective just as with court jesters and politics.   Not because there is nothing sacred, but because we need to distinguish what's sacred from our sacred cows.   As long as we are good listeners, baptizing all manner of religiosity in laughter can be effective.   It can even tear down idols erected in the place of God.

---

[3] Ibid. (Comments section).

Colbert once commented, "I try not to make jokes about someone's religion for what the religion *is* but for the abuse of that religion."[4]

God is not the butt of the joke. The things people do in God's name are the target. The ungodly things we associate with God are fair game for mockery.

CROSSING THE LINE

This can get tricky. How do we draw a line between jokes about religion and mocking God? Religious belief is personal and serious. Getting infected by uncontrollable giggles in church is one thing. That can garner stern looks from senior members. But willfully poking fun of sacred things?

Our gut might tell us it's inappropriate to recklessly joke about religion. Insert the old line about not standing too close to a blasphemer for fear of a lightning strike. It simply seems more seemly when all manner of God-talk maintains gravitas and solemnity.

This follows a cultural logic. Children are taught to be respectful toward parents, teachers, and the Queen of England (should they have the strange fortune to meet her). The level of respect and decorum increases proportionately with the perceived importance of the person.

---

[4] *The Paul Mecurio Show* (#26) interview with Stephen Colbert on August 12, 2013. Podcast URL:
http://sideshownetwork.tv/podcastsEpisode.cfm?podcastid=68&episodeID=2659

Sassiness with a teacher is more easily forgiven than anything short of perfect manners in the presence of the Queen. It stands to reason, therefore, that when we sing songs, rehearse words, or perform rites invoking the presence of the Creator and Sustainer of All Things that deep reverence is required.

It's not that people believe God is uptight or against humor. He *created* laughter and mirth. He turns mourning into dancing. But nobody wants to be a blasphemer. If ever restraint should be exercised it is concerning "God stuff." There are lines of propriety with regard to the sacred that should not be crossed.

But where is the line and how do we draw it?

Asked that very question, Stephen Colbert matter-of-factly stated, "I don't make fun of the Eucharist or the Passion. That's a line for me."[5]

Producing shows four times a week with a team of writers attempting to jam pack every minute with jokes, Colbert acknowledged it might be possible to locate an instance of him breaking that rule. Nevertheless, Jesus on the cross and the holy meal of remembrance Colbert deemed "too far."

Limits exist, and a level of respect is appropriate. But good religious humor does not empty serious matters of their seriousness, it exposes absurdities that attach themselves to serious matters. When "things of God" are declared off limits in the name of reverence and respect, any number of ignoble "things" can sneak by in the name of God, calling us to revere the unrespectable.

---

[5] Ibid.

Consider how politicians sneak "pork" into a bill of law.   They offer something you want but deliver it with something you don't (a concession to greed or special interests) and demand that you accept the whole package.   The stated purpose of a bill can be a respectable foil for junk snuck in the back pages.

In the same way, religion can be a perfect cover for doing or saying things that are ungodly while claiming immunity on account of God's name.   Comedy can adeptly expose this dissonance.

Claims of immunity under the guise of reverence are yet another reason comedy must be licensed to operate without consequences.   The problem is not that we have an overabundance of reverence for God, the problem is that "things" that are not of God are allowed to thrive unchecked by sneaking under the umbrella of godly reverence.   When we make religious things too sacred to talk or laugh about we effectively erect idols out of those religious things.

We can even make an idol out of God.   How?   By taking something which is not God or godly and attributing it to God.

For example, if we claim God is distant, vindictive, or apathetic we construct a false god and thus, an idol in the name of God. Such gods can be exposed by philosophical discourse or theological argument...

Also through "irreverent" humor.[6]

---

[6] NT Wright, former Bishop of Durham and one time guest on The Colbert Report argues that the best answer to the question of whether or not one believes in God is to retort, "Which god?"   He further asserts that our Western conception of God is often more reflective of Deism than biblical.   We imagine God as a distant landlord who has more

Too much reverence can have unintended consequences. For example, one way to adhere to the Third Commandment (which forbids taking the LORD's name in vain) is to never speak the Name at all. A person can avoid speaking foolishly about God by never speaking of God.

You could call this extreme reverence. Or you could call this missing the point. Especially if you understand the command as belonging to a greater framework aimed at intimacy and relationship with God.

The intention of "the Law" can be subverted by reverence.

Even when the object of our reverence is inherently good or holy, over-zealous reverence can skew our perspective to the point of idolatry.

Another example. Consider the Bible on your bookshelf (you *do* have a Bible don't you?). Suppose you are reaching to get a vase off the top shelf but you are a little too short (or vertically challenged). What would you think of putting *The Holy Bible* on the floor and stepping on it with your street-stomping shoes to extend your reach? Does this cross a line?

Many would *not* step on their sacred text for such a pedestrian cause as securing a vessel to stage the dandelions their kids picked. However, this mindset flirts with a magical and even idolatrous way of thinking - a way of thinking that is countered in nearly every page of the text we refuse to stand upon.

---

or less checked out and isn't overly involved in our world. This is not a Christian vision of God and is a god that should be summarily rejected – through comedy or otherwise!

It is not the ink or the paper or the leather binding that is sacred, it is the One to whom its authors bore faithful witness in its pages and chapters.

Abundant care and diligence to avoid blasphemy can backfire and make us blasphemers. If we treat the Bible as equal to God instead of the text that reveals God we are guilty of magical and pagan thinking. It is akin to grabbing an artifact Jesus might have touched or picking some piece of creation where God's fingerprint can be discerned and elevating it to an object of worship. The Bible word is idolatry.

A map that describes mountains, hills, roads, and rivers is not the land itself – it's just a map. In the case of the Bible, the book is neither a deity nor a "roadmap" for life. Scripture is where we get introduced to the Guide who alone is worthy of worship.

Scripture itself forbids idols and images of any kind. Jews and Christians were viewed suspiciously in the first century for what was unheard of among the pagans – imageless worship. The profound insight was that nothing whatsoever is holy. Better yet, that *all* things are holy because they are made by a holy Creator. We ourselves bear the image of that Creator (and should treat each other accordingly).

When "stuff" (even good stuff like the Bible, doctrines, songs, and baptismal water) is over-revered, "stuff" becomes an end in itself as opposed to pointing Godward like holy "stuff" is supposed to.

The distinction between objects and the Object of faith is critical. Comedy pokes at sacred beliefs and demands we question whether what we revere is truth, the gospel, God… or only constructions of these.

BLITZKRIEG

One telling example of irreverence on *The Colbert Report* is the recurring Christmas segment "The Blitzkrieg On Grinchitude."

The segment opens with a graphic cartoon. Santa Claus is flying through the sky pulled by reindeer in his sleigh full of presents. Alas, a red WWI fighter plane invades and the enemy of Christmas shoots down Santa's vessel. Santa falls from his sleigh, downward through the night sky. Just in time, none other than Jesus himself arrives flying a blue bi-plane and catches Santa in the back seat. Complete with goggles and scarf, the cartoon Jesus turns to the camera and gives a thumbs up. Jesus saves Christmas.[7]

The parody packed news story following the cartoon typically involves a complaint about the celebration of Christmas in America being subverted by "Holiday" mongers and "Season" greeters. Clips from Fox News December coverage are highlighted reporting instances of nativity scenes being removed or "Merry Christmas" greetings being forbidden. "The Blitzkrieg On Grinchitude" parodies Fox's coverage.

Fox News may have a valid point criticizing our overly "PC" culture and hyper-phobia concerning any kind of religious expression – especially Christian. Still, Colbert's "Blitzkrieg" is a prime example of how parody functions – questioning

---

[7] For example, episode 1282, aired December 11, 2013.

assumptions and challenging viewers to reflect on the differences between God and our constructions in God's name.

No one in their right mind believes Jesus is a Santa-rescuing pilot patrolling the skies of America for the sake of Christmas. It is precisely this false portrayal that invites us to discern what is *not* false.   By casting Jesus as "Defender of Christmas," the cartoon and the segment to follow make the satirical claim that Jesus' followers do likewise.

To be a Jesus-follower, according to the parody, is to oppose vehemently the holidayification™ of Christmas.

The parody insinuates what needs "saving" is not the remembrance of Christ's incarnation, Bethlehem, or the manger but Santa Claus - the red-suited cultural idol along with the consumerism and marketing he represents. The implied question asks; Is the religiously motivated defense of "Christ" in Christmas is really interested in Christ at all?

Similar, and potentially more-offensive, is the segment "Easter Under Attack" on *The Colbert Report*. This bit features cartoon Jesus shot at and returning gunfire from behind the rock of The Empty Tomb.[8]

The ensuing "story" usually involves complaints about the lack of freedom to celebrate Easter in today's politically correct public square. The real tragedy, according to the parody, is being deprived of chocolate and Easter bunnies. Conspicuously missing from the "coverage" is what Easter is actually about. The resurrection of Jesus.

---

[8] A great example is episode 865, aired April 14, 2011

The absence, of course, is precisely the thing to notice.[9]   The parody casts Jesus as defensive, violent, and combative against the tide of culture.   It suggests that defending Easter in the name of Jesus is less about a desire to spread the hope of resurrection and more about preserving a threatened cultural identity in an increasingly post-Christian America.

In 2014, Colbert reported that churches at Easter were resorting to various marketing techniques, "Thankfully, this year some churches began spending money on gifts and prizes in hopes of boosting attendance on Easter Sunday.   At last! Prizes!   I mean what else were they going to lure people in with?   The promise of unconditional love and eternal salvation?   They gave that out last year."[10]

The false portrayal of Jesus as a cartoon character acting not-very-Jesus-like should not offend us.   If we turn off the TV in disgust, we miss a conversation worth having.   The caricature is false, but the falsehood stirs a curiosity and longing for a Jesus who transcends caricature.   Portraying Jesus absurdly on *The Colbert Report* implies a contrast with the Jesus not mentioned.   The appropriate response to the parody is to compare the caricature with the reality and then ask ourselves which one we most resemble.

Parody is a mirror of truth.

A cartoon Jesus shooting a gun from The Empty Tomb should inspire viewers to reason, "That is *not* what Jesus is like.   Jesus

---

[9] This reminds me of the Sherlock Holmes who called attention to the curious incident of the dog barking in the night.   A Scotland Yard detective protested that the dog did not bark in the night.   "That is what was curious," replied Sherlock Holmes.

[10] Episode 1338, aired April 21, 2014

is not violent. Jesus is full of self-emptying love. Jesus is not threatened or defensive. Jesus is the one who endured oppression while forgiving and praying for his enemies. How, then, as followers of Jesus can we strive to be more like the Jesus of Scripture and less like a cartoon?"

If parody is prohibited, we might go on imagining that despising those who oppose our point of view is Jesus-like. The irreverent cartoon and satirical Jesus create space for an authentic encounter with the real Jesus. The parody declares what is false about Jesus. But if it's forbidden, anything false in the name of Jesus is allowed to go unchecked.

WOULD THE REAL JESUS PLEASE STAND UP

Awful things are done in the name of religion. Money scandals, sex scandals, and abuse happen in churches and religious institutions with alarming frequency. Not all who claim the name of Jesus look or act anything like him. Simply claiming that God is on our side does not make it so.

This is as true today as it was in the European wars where fighters slew each other under different colored banners hailing the one true Prince of Peace. Applying the name of Jesus to any given part of God's creation does not make it any more Jesus-like than it was before.

Misrepresentations of Jesus by fringe groups like Westoboro Baptist are obvious and overt. Subtle distortions can be harder to recognize.

In America, Jesus is cast in a myriad of ways. Are we to believe the image of a muscle bound savior on the T-shirts which read "God's Gym: His Pain, Your Gain"?   Are we to believe the pictures of a blue-eyed Anglo in a white robe carrying a sheep on his shoulders?   Are we to accept the theories touted by scholars on television shows when they try out new, controversial angles uncovering the "real" Jesus of history?

Competing and contradictory versions of Jesus make discernment crucial.

Why would anyone want to distort or recreate Jesus?

It's not always sinister or malicious.   It's said that God made human beings in his image and we've been trying to return the compliment ever since.   Bible scholars often note with amusement how biographers of Jesus have a tendency to imagine Jesus very much like themselves.

Re-casting Jesus to fit with our agendas is natural.   It is much easier than repenting or being transformed to look more like him.[11]   Changing our way of thinking, living, and being is enormously difficult.   Tweaking religious understandings is relatively easy.   As the saying goes, "Broad is the way that leadeth to destruction."[12]

Another saying is that if you dance with the devil, the devil doesn't change, the devil changes you.   The inverse is not

---

[11] The meaning of the word repentance, μετανοια, in the New Testament has to do with changing one's mind or turning and going in a different direction.
[12] Matthew 7:13, KJV *The Holy Bible: King James Version.* (2009). (Electronic Edition of the 1900 Authorized Version., Lk 24:37–38). Bellingham, WA: Logos Research Systems, Inc.

true.[13]   God and all things holy are regularly co-opted for the sake of marketability, selfish interests, and ungodly agendas.

This can happen on a subtle, individual level.   I want my faith in God and Jesus to function as implicit endorsement for my priorities, accustomed lifestyle, and social allegiances.   I do not want to be challenged or undermined.

This can also happen on a large scale with organizations, institutions, and societies.   A willingness to change what we mean when we say "God" is easier than repentance or changing how we operate in the world.   Especially when our comfort is involved.   Especially when our definitions of "good" and "bad," "us" and "them" are threatened.

SUBJECTED TO FIRE

When things we hold dear get trampled by jokes, feelings are bound to be hurt.   Nevertheless, subjecting our beliefs and practices to comedic inquiry is a hurt that we religious types would do well to endure.   Like the Apostle Paul said in 1 Corinthians 3, Christ is the foundation, but what we build upon that foundation is bound to be tested by fire.[14]

Religious beliefs are sacred.   The risk of being shocked or offended when comedy pokes at religion increases exponentially.   It can be difficult to experience our deepest

---

[13] Actually the inverse *is* true.   We become like what we worship, as argued in Chapter Five.   Worshipping the One True God in Jesus transforms us to look like Jesus.   Nevertheless, there is no shortage of constructs of God and Jesus which do not bear God's likeness which is the point of this section.

[14]   1 Corinthians 3:10-15

held fears, hopes, and beliefs treated lightly, on the one hand, or overly scrutinized on the other.

Psychoanalysis is surely correct in asserting that the things that rile us up and provoke a reaction reveal a sensitive nerve. When offended, the crucial question is, "Why does this offend me?   What is it about my beliefs and way of being in this world that make this scandalous?   God is not threatened or diminished… So why am I?   Is there a doubt or conflict in myself I don't want to face?"

Rude comics are not exempt from being declared rude. Comics should be exempt from consequences, but that does not mean we should accept or agree with everything (or even one single thing) they say.

But we *should* examine our reactions.

Jokes about religion or flippant references to symbols, practices, and institutions associated with our religious beliefs can seem offensive and derogatory.   Jokes about religion can feel out of place - like party hats at a funeral or Bermuda shorts at a formal dinner.   But *why* they affect us or ruffle our feathers is a more telling line of inquiry than the motivation of the joke-teller.

The jester's role is to provoke, our role is to discern.

The angelic exhortation, "Do not be afraid" is perpetually appropriate.   Parrhesia should be continually be evoked.   If God is not threatened in Jesus unlikely sinners are granted grace, free speech, and license to approach the throne of God as God-welcomed and beloved…   Let freedom reign!

Let the jokes fly, let the scoffers scoff, let the truth be true. There are worse things than being offended.   There are worse things than being made an object of ridicule.   Remember that by the cross of Roman-inflicted shame Jesus made a "public spectacle" of the powers and principalities.[15]

Only by openness and freedom without consequences can we arrive at the truth.   Like a co-dependent nuclear family where tensions lurk beneath the surface of every discourse, only by honestly and lovingly laying everything on the table is there a chance of healing and wholeness.   The same goes for religion.

The reason Jesus jokes are funny is that they strip us of vain imaginations of who God is and how belief functions and leave us longing for what is authentic.   When we give up our constructions of God we think we can't do without we are left with our desire for who we really need.

God, revealed in Jesus.

---

[15] Colossians 2:15

8.

Banqueting Table

"You prepare a table before me in the presence of my enemies"

Psalm 23:5[1]

TABLE FELLOWSHIP

Six minutes.

This is the typical time allotment afforded guests in the last segment of *The Colbert Report*. For some, those six minutes are a time to shine, show off, or experience the coveted Colbert Bump.[2] For others, it is an unbearable and awkward eternity to endure. For still others, it is an agitating and utterly confusing madness.

---

[1] Psalm 23:5 *The Holy Bible: New Revised Standard Version*. (1989). Nashville: Thomas Nelson Publishers.
[2] The "Colbert Bump" is the real or perceived boost that a guest on *The Colbert Report* receives promoting their book, topic, movie, etc.

All manner of musicians, authors, actors, politicians, enter-tainers, military personnel, professors, and public intellectuals have sat across the table from Stephen Colbert.   Colbert has hosted various people for mini-interviews at his news desk, he's streamed guests "live via satellite," he's worked guests into comedy bits, and of course, *The Colbert Report* has featured many musical performances.   But the tried and true platform for featuring outside voices has been the six minute interview near the end of the show when Colbert declares, "My guest tonight…"

Just like on *The Daily Show, The Late Show,* or for that matter, *The View,* when a guest's name is announced the live studio audience cheers and applauds.   If the guest is relatively un-known the applause is supportive but moderate.   If the guest is an A-list actor, a musical legend, or some other breed of superstar the reception is fanatic and deafening.

On *The Colbert Report,* Stephen announces the name of his guest but makes the presumptuous assumption that the ensuing applause and adoration is directed to him and him alone.   The host leaps down from his desk, parades across his set, high fives his audience, bows, blows kisses, and holds his hands outstretched like an Olympic champion who just won gold.

Amid this pomp and circumstance, Colbert does not so much as glance in the direction of his guest.   His back remains toward them until, finally, he takes his seat at the table where they are already sitting and waiting.   He shakes hands and welcomes them as if to say, "Sorry, they just can't get enough of my greatness.   Now I've carved out a moment for you.   By extension the audience has carved out a moment for you.   But let's not forget it is me, Stephen Colbert, who is the center."

This ritualized humbling is only the beginning of the challenge Colbert's guests face.   Stephen Colbert can dial his character "way down" if the interview calls for it.   As he said himself, "If I feel like the person is really nervous, I dial it back immediately, so they can feel comfortable."

Nevertheless, he can dial it "way up" such that the interview is a rollicking roller coaster ride.

Colbert makes it a policy to meet with guests out of character prior to taping an episode.   He asks whether they are familiar with the show and makes it clear that the person they will meet on camera is not the same person they meet before the show.

"I tell people before the show begins, 'Hey ... I do the show in character, and he's an idiot, and he's willfully ignorant of what you know and care about. Please just honestly disabuse me of my ignorance. Don't let me put words in your mouth, and we'll have a great time out there.'"[3]

THE HOT SEAT

Barbara Walters is known for making guests cry.[4]   James Lipton, on *Inside the Actors Studio*, never fails to ask, "If heaven

---

[3] "Colbert: 'RE-Becoming the Nation We Always Were" on *Fresh Air* with Terry Gross on NPR.   URL: http://www.npr.org/2012/10/04/162304439/colbert-re-becoming-the-nation-we-always-were

[4] For example, URL: http://www.boston.com/news/nation/2014/05/13/barbara-walters-makes-celebrities-cry-lot/H46u1pJNXNKvAGfqPZAutJ/story.html

exists, what would you like to hear God say when you arrive at the pearly gates?"[5]

A straight question deserves a straight answer. But how do you prepare for an interview with a complete phony? What is it like to sit in the chair and hear your name announced by Stephen Colbert?

"My guest tonight is the co-founder of Twitter. I'll ask him every mundane detail about every moment of his life. Please welcome Biz Stone."[6]

"My guest tonight is a director, who at the age of 26 directed his first feature film which has now been nominated for four Oscars. I will pretend that I'm happy for him."[7]

"My guest tonight is David Brooks. He's a moderate conservative and a columnist for the *New York Times*. I'll ask him what it's like to be in two dying industries at once."[8]

Author Jennifer 8. Lee was a guest on *The Report* which inspired her to write an article, "How Do You Survive an Interview on *The Colbert Report?*" The best advice she got beforehand was, "Just be calm and roll with the weirdness."[9]

---

[5] James Lipton's ten questions can be viewed on any episode of *Inside the Actor's Studio* and are listed at the following post. URL: http://en.wikipedia.org/wiki/Inside_the_Actors_Studio

[6] Episode 535, aired April 2, 2009

[7] Episode 1150, aired February 7, 2013 (featuring Benh Zeitlin).

[8] Episode 682, aired March 2, 2010

[9] Rachel Axler quoted by Jennifer 8. Lee on Quora.com Reposted URL: http://www.slate.com/blogs/quora/2014/04/08/how_do_you_survive_an_interview_with_stephen_colbert_on_the_colbert_report.html

Sparring with a sharp witted comedian and satirist can be intimidating even if you understand the game – especially under studio lights with cameras rolling and people everywhere watching.

Lee prepared studiously for her interview.   Her 2008 appearance went well.   Her Golden Rule was, "Don't try to be funny."[10]

When guests attempt to be sarcastic, satirical, or out-Colbert Colbert, interviews veer into the unfunny.   When guests are simply themselves and patiently put up with dumb questions as though talking to an idiot, things go well and the voice of the guest is heard.

Satire needs a "straight man."   For exaggeration to work, it needs to have a reference point in reality.   At Colbert's interview table, the guest is the ground of reality which allows the comic to soar to exaggerated heights and give viewers perspective over the landscape.   The guest's voice is amplified by the buffoon if they do exactly what he asks.   Namely, disabuse him of his ignorance.   If the guest tries to match buffoonery with buffoonery, the whole game falls apart and the interview (as well as the comedy) falls flat.

WHAT THE HELL ARE YOU TALKING ABOUT?

Interviews with Colbert go sideways when guests fail to "get the memo" that Stephen Colbert does his show in character.

---

[10] Jennifer 8. Lee on Quora.com   Reposted URL:
http://www.slate.com/blogs/quora/2014/04/08/how_do_you_survive_a_n_interview_with_stephen_colbert_on_the_colbert_report.html

The willful ignorance of Colbert's character looms large enough that if a guest doesn't get the joke or understand they are entering a context of pure fakery they will be left shocked and confused.

For example, when an African American guest comes on the program to discuss race, Colbert usually begins his interview by asking them if they are black. He follows with the explanation, "I don't see race. People tell me that I'm white and I believe them…"

If the satirical context is not understood, such a statement is absurd and confusing. From time to time, pure confusion is witnessed on *The Report.*

On *Meet the* Press, Colbert recalled an early interview with Senator Bob Kerrey who was making his rounds on the press circuit as a result of his work on the 9/11 Commission Report. He was completely unaware of Stephen's character and *The Colbert Report* as a satirical comedy show. Three minutes into the interview he turned to Colbert bewildered and angrily growled, "What the hell are you talking about?"

Colbert, of course, would not break character. His guest suffered through.[11]

Awkwardness can be funny but also difficult to watch. When Colbert docs field interviews on *The Colbert Report* (as he did regularly as a correspondent on *The Daily Show*) it is awkwardness that drives the comedy. The recurring segment, "Difference Makers," for example, highlights and celebrates

---

[11] On *Meet the Press* with David Gregory on NBC, published October 14, 2012. URL:
http://www.nbcnews.com/video/meet-the-press/49407301

people doing things that are absurd, irresponsible, or just plain bad with unmitigated passion.   Colbert interviews the person, identifies with them completely, and champions their flatly unworthy cause.

In June, 2014 "Difference Makers" featured a Florida man who transformed his backyard into a firing range.   In his mind, his legal right to fire his weapons trumped all external circumstances (like the fact that he lived on a well trafficked canal and his neighbors were understandably outraged at his refusal to go to a nearby shooting range for the sake of safety).

"There's nothing illegal about me shooting in my backyard. Even if there is a boat and a kid... I don't care."[12]

Colbert took the side of the reckless shooter, praising him as a freedom fighter persecuted by narrow minded neighbors who clearly hated America.   The effect on the viewer, on the one hand, is disbelief.   Does this kind of lunacy actually exist?

On the other hand, viewers are left to puzzle about the "Difference Makers" themselves. Can they really take themselves seriously?   Do they not *get* that their cause is the joke itself?   Why would they agree to go on a show like this?

"Difference Makers" celebrated by Colbert have included a man who made it a policy to give the middle finger to every police officer he encountered; the builder of a web site for women to get free breast implants; a pastor who shut down a seniors social gathering for fear that BINGO games were a slippery slope to serious crime; a woman who equated teaching

---

[12] Episode 1358, aired June 2, 2014

pole dancing to feminism; and a lawyer who wanted to sue bars for having Ladies Night.

"If they want equality let's give them 51% of the worst of our society. Then they'll change their tune and start whining, 'Where's the kitchen?'"[13]

The rich supply of people willing to stand up for absurd causes on *The Colbert Report* is part of the same phenomena that can be observed on reality TV shows. On *The Bachelor*, *American Idol*, *Survivor*, *Real Housewives* or any other such show it seems that countless people are willing to put their lives in front of cameras and embarrass themselves, air their dirty laundry, display their cruelty, or otherwise make fools of themselves on national television.

Philosopher Peter Rollins had an insight, "People do reality TV because no one thinks they're an idiot. You've got a vested interest in thinking you're cool because you hang around with yourself all the time. But you need someone else sometimes in order to see yourself."[14]

The moral of the story? If cameras, an interview crew, and a renowned satirist arrive at your home or place of work taking

---

[13] Robert Ekas, who flips the bird to police was featured in Episode 711, which aired April 28, 2010. Pastor Larry Johnson who shut down BINGO was featured in Episode 1044, which aired June 6, 2012. Jason Grunstra who launched www.myfreeimplants.com was featured in Episode 361, which aired March 5, 2008. Johanna Mink and her pole-dancing school was featured in Episode 282, which aired July 16, 2007. Anti-feminist attorney Roy Den Hollander and the above quote were featured in Episode 857, which aired on March 31, 2011.
[14] Peter Rollins, lecture at Central Avenue Church, Glendale, CA on March 15, 2014. Posted on YouTube at https://www.youtube.com/watch?v=6xA8bpcqWrA

your cause entirely seriously, it is cause for alarm and time to rethink your cause.

LIGHT + TRUTH = EXPOSURE

This was the insight of House Speaker Nancy Pelosi in 2006 when she advised Democrats against doing interviews with Stephen Colbert.   Colbert was conducting hilarious interviews with every ilk of politician for his 434 part "Better Know a District" series.   Pelosi saw all too well how absurdity shone the light of truth: "I watch it all the time and I think, 'Why would anybody go on there?'"[15]

One cautionary tale was Congressman Lynn Westmoreland who went on the show earlier in 2006 supporting a bill for the display of the Bible's Ten Commandments on historic courthouse sites – a slam dunk conservative stance for a conservative politician.   Colbert asked the obvious question, "What are The Ten Commandments?"

Westmoreland was taken off guard, "What are all of them? You want me to name them all?"   Colbert nodded. Embarrassed, Westmoreland struggled to come up with three.[16]

Thou Shalt Not Submit to Interviews with Stephen Colbert.

At least, not if transparency will hurt your cause.

---

[15] "Running for office? Better run from Stephen Colbert" by Jim Puzzanghera, *LA Times* online, October 22, 2006. URL: http://articles.latimes.com/2006/oct/22/business/fi-colbert22
[16] Ibid, Cf. Episode 106, aired June 14, 2006.

Nancy Pelosi eventually appeared on *The Colbert Report* in 2012 and "okayed" other Democrats to do the same.[17] Still, her previous caution was neither unwise nor unfounded. Comedy can bring out inconvenient facts. Like ignorance concerning The Ten Commandments. It can also expose character faults.

Segments like "Difference Makers" or "Better Know a District" are funny but also agonizing to watch when the person being interviewed allows themselves to become the joke. Colbert's persistent ignorance is precisely what brings out the ignorance of the subject. Watching is painful because it is "laughing-at-you-not-laughing-with-you" comedy.

Is this kind of comedy just mean?

This is an important tension. Damaging a person in the sense of undermining their worth as a beloved and precious human being made in the image of God is wrong. However, coaxing out harmful ideas or hypocritical stances, exposing them to the light, and showing them for what they are is part of the burden that comedy carries - the burden of truth telling.

When I watched Colbert's interview with Westmoreland I laughed hard but couldn't help feeling bad for the man who became the butt of the joke. I assume he is a decent human being with real feelings that no doubt were hurt by Colbert's show. He probably experienced shame and anger as a result of being interviewed. He wasn't trapped but he was definitely

---

[17] "Nancy Pelosi Succumbs to the Power of Colbert" by Sophia A. McClennen, *Huffington Post Politics*, The Blog, February 24, 2012. URL: http://www.huffingtonpost.com/sophia-a-mcclennen/nancy-pelosi-suc cumbs-to- b 1299738.html

"set up."   And he was certainly walking into something that he was not prepared for.   I couldn't help feeling bad for him.

Nevertheless, the interview turned on a light and exposed something true.   What did it expose?   The gap between what politicians say and what they do; the hollowness in claims of deeply held convictions and values; the brokenness of our political system and a Congress who can't pass bills even though both sides of the argument can't even articulate the content of their own arguments.

If you stand up and declare that target shooting next to crowded canals is a good idea you subject your claim to a counter argument.   If you publicly declare that teaching pole dancing is equivalent to feminism you have opened a door to public criticism.   Free speech demands free criticism and somebody to call, "Foul!"

For the sake of anyone who might be duped by strange ideas, someone has to tell the truth.   Satire can sting, but its aim is truth.

For a third time, rude comics should be declared rude. However, like in journalism, avoiding hurting someone's feelings is not a good enough reason to suppress a story or suppress the truth.   On the flip side, having hurt feelings as a result of being exposed (as wrong, ridiculous, or both) is an opportunity for the offended to give up credibility and become a more honest and authentic human being.

COME TO THE TABLE

Colbert, himself, has acknowledged that being subjected to his character's interviews is not easy. "It can be a difficult booking," he said.[18]

"It is one thing to appreciate comedy as a spectator but," Colbert continued, "it is another thing when you actually get out there, and I am aggressively *dumb* at you... I'm very grateful for anyone who would come into that odd arena — especially someone who doesn't know the show or isn't a fan of the show."[19]

In contrast to when Colbert is in the field, he has a lot of grace for guests at his own interview table. "I'm not an assassin," Colbert insists.[20]

His aim is not "take down" his guests – even when he disagrees with them.   Instead, Colbert likens his interviews on the show to "trying to keep the balloon in the air."[21]

[18] On *Meet the Press* with David Gregory on NBC, published October 14, 2012.   URL:
http://www.nbcnews.com/video/meet-the-press/49407301
[19] "Colbert: 'RE-Becoming the Nation We Always Were" on *Fresh Air* with Terry Gross on NPR.   URL:
http://www.npr.org/2012/10/04/162304439/colbert-re-becoming-the-n ation-we-always-were
[20] "Colbert: 'RE-Becoming the Nation We Always Were" on *Fresh Air* with Terry Gross on NPR.   URL:
http://www.npr.org/2012/10/04/162304439/colbert-re-becoming-the-n ation-we-always-were
[21] "The Playboy Interview: Stephen Colbert on Politics, Grief and Bill O'Reilly" by Eric Spitznagel, originally published in *Playboy*, November 2012, posted online April 10, 2014.   URL:
http://playboysfw.kinja.com/the-playboy-interview-stephen-colbert-on-politics-gri-1561831379

"I look at every guest *as* a guest," Colbert explained, "they're a guest in my home, and I am grateful that they would come… I actually do want people to have a good time."

The entire staff of *The Colbert Report* refer to the show's creation and production as "The Joy Machine."   Colbert revels in the diversity of voices he has heard – the variety of thought, talent, and character he has had the privilege to interact and engage with.   His favorite guest, he said, is one who is genuinely passionate about the book or idea they are promoting.[22]

At the same time, people *want* to be on the show.   Even politicians who have been warned (and ought to know better) are eager to come on the show and defy the risk of looking foolish.   The joy associated with "The Joy Machine" is evident from afar.   People like to be in the presence of joy and revel in the idea of sitting across the table from Stephen Colbert.

TABLE FELLOWSHIP

It may seem like a furious leap from the interview table on the set of *The Colbert Report* to the sacred table of fellowship between human beings as brothers and sisters together with their Creator.   But the former is at least a hint of the latter.

Consider the metaphor and symbol of the table.   The table is the place for eating – a universal and cross-cultural expression of being human.

---

[22] "Ken Burns in Conversation with Stephen Colbert,"   Events at the Apple Store presented by Apple, Inc.   February 14, 2014.   Podcast: https://itunes.apple.com/us/podcast/ken-burns-in-conversation/id8216 98225?mt=2

Table is where humans connect and engage with one another. Table stands for laughter and for truth.   It's hard to sit at table with an enemy.

Table is also a symbol of enormous importance in Scripture. Table fellowship was the means of expressing peace and reconciliation in the Old Testament as well as the place where covenants were ratified.

In the New Testament, most of Jesus teachings were delivered in the context of a meal.

In the first century, "going to church" was synonymous with gathering at a table and sharing a meal.

In the book of Revelation, heaven is inaugurated by a meal – restored table fellowship between God and human beings made possible in Jesus.[23]

Very short of the Bible's lavish vision of table fellowship in Christ is the interview table on *The Colbert Report*.   Still, it is the place on the show where there is grace, a measure of hospitality, and space for a variety of voices.   At Colbert's table there are rivers of joy if you have a sense of humor.

And also truth.

Truth can hurt our feelings, expose our shortcomings, and shine the light on our absurdities as it so often does on *The Report*.   In this sense, Colbert's table is dangerous.

Risk notwithstanding, the table points to a fundamental human desire.   We all desire a place to come where our voice is heard,

---

[23] Technically, in the book of Revelation "heaven" already exists but what is inaugurated is "the new heavens and the new earth."

where our unique being and existence is acknowledged, where our absurdity, weakness, meanness, and even badness is exposed but we are nevertheless accepted as beloved, precious human beings made in the image of God.

The gospel is the invitation to God's table, fulfilling our hope and craving for parrhesia.

Free to speak, free to be, free of the fear of condemnation. Accepted yet authentic, connected in fellowship with humanity, connected likewise with God. Loved, and granted a seat at the table.

9.

The Priesthood of All Comics

"But you are a chosen people, a royal priesthood."

1 Peter 2:9[1]

VENGEFUL MONKEYS

"Okay, let's explain to the kids out there that God *does* exist, that God *does* love you. Because their image of God from the MTVs and the Nintendos is like some vengeful monkey who's throwing barrels at Super Mario. They don't know who God is. Who *is* God, Rick?"[2]

Colbert sat across from Rick Warren, America's most widely read mega-church pastor promoting his book *The Purpose Driven Life*. Colbert was snappy, quick, and dialed up. For most questions, Warren's first response was laugh. Instead of waiting for an answer, Colbert just fired more questions.

---

[1] 1 Peter 2:9a *The New International Version*. (2011). Grand Rapids, MI: Zondervan
[2] Episode 344, aired January 28, 2008

For this one, however, Warren managed to give a response.

"God is creator," said Warren. After describing the unique conditions by which the existence of this world is possible he concluded, "[God] wanted to create human beings. He wanted to create you to love you. He loves even Stephen Colbert."

"Oh I believe that," replied Colbert, "He created me in his image and I sure love me."

Rick Warren's definition of God was not theologically comprehensive (not to mention somewhat anthropocentric). But it's not a bad start for the "kids out there" with a "vengeful monkey" image of God. Moreover, Warren's book focuses on human vocation and purpose and the author made it clear that simplicity was his goal.

Colbert continued, "The sub-question of the book is 'What on earth am I here for?' What do you think the purpose of life is? Is it individual, or do you believe in something like the Baltimore catechism that we're here to know God, to love God, to serve God?"

What makes being interviewed by Stephen Colbert difficult and exciting is that while his character is an ignoramus; the actor behind him is all too knowledgeable – especially when it comes to religion. A guest like Rick Warren has to be quick on his feet with an interlocutor who at one moment likens God to a game of Donkey Kong and the next is quoting Roman Catholic catechisms.

Colbert's question was a good one. What *is* the purpose of life?

The fact that Rick Warren's book is one of the bestselling books of all time would indicate the question is alive and relevant.[3]   According to Colbert, the voice of the market should always be heeded.   In the case of *The Purpose Driven Life*, over 30 million copies in worldwide sales shout rather loudly; people want to know and connect with their purpose.

Clarifying the distinctions between a corporate and individual understanding of purpose proved to be too much for the scope of Colbert's six minute interview with Rick Warren.   Late night talk show interviews are typically promotional teasers.

In this case, connecting the purpose of life to the identity of God and the logic of creation was an effective teaser not just for Warren's book, but for the question of purpose itself. Purpose and human vocation are not just matters for Rick Warren, Stephen Colbert, and 30 million readers – it's a fundamental human issue.

VOCATION

Vocation is a word that refers to calling, identity, and purpose in life.   In our culture, introductions at a backyard barbecue typically involve the question, "What do you do for a living?" Vocation, however, is not equivalent to career, profession, or "day job."   They can certainly be linked, but vocation connotes identity and purpose transcending a paycheck.

---

[3] *The Purpose Driven Life* has sold over 30 million copies and been translated into 56 different languages according to Wikipedia's referenced entry on List of Best-Selling Books. URL: http://en.wikipedia.org/wiki/List_of_best-selling_books

Better than asking "What do you do for a living?" might be "What is the divinely appointed work for which you were put on this earth?"   But don't blame me if you scare people off in casual conversation.

The following is a brief theological sketch concerning the purpose of life as priestly, the purpose of comedy as priestly, and the priesthood of all believers as it extends to the comic.

VOCATIONAL THEOLOGY 101

In Christian theology, Christ is often talked about as having a threefold vocation; Prophet, Priest, and King.   Fulfilling these vocations is related to Christ's divinity but at the same time related to God's establishment of Jesus as the true human, or, as Paul put it, the "Second Adam."[4]   In Christ, the human identity lost in the Fall of the first Adam is restored.

In the aftermath of this restoration (i.e. post-resurrection existence) human beings are no longer to live in the brokenness of the first Adam.   Scripture urges us to find our being "in Christ," living out our *human* vocation within *Christ's* vocation.   1 John 4:18 emphasizes, "As he is, so are we in this world."   Broadly speaking, the Christian understanding of human vocation is to be as Christ in this world.

Christ is Prophet, Priest, and King and we are called to be the same.

King, in the sense that we carry the commission bestowed on humanity in the Garden of Eden to fill the earth and subdue it.

---

[4] 1 Corinthians 15:45

This "dominion" is not about the right to club baby seals or burn Styrofoam.   It's the call to participate in God's project of tending the garden of creation increasingly in keeping with God's inbreaking kingdom in which all powers, principalities, and existence are rightly ordered under his reign.

Prophet, in the sense that we are called to listen to God.   To hear the truth and speak the truth, identify our idols, and cast an enticing vision of God's life and goodness.   The prophet calls creation to abandon loveless and non-relational modes of being that lead to death and embrace the new creation of God's reign in Christ which is life.

Priest, in the sense that...   Priesthood is a much larger category.   The category of priesthood envelops that of King and Prophet.

PRIESTS

Vocational theology might not be funny or fun to talk about. It may be amusing and ironic that I'm seeking to identify the Catholic comic Stephen Colbert and his comedy as "priestly."

The very Protestant doctrine of "Universal Priesthood" was no small part of the issue at stake in the sixteenth century when the Protestants split off from "The One True Church" Colbert belongs to.   But almost every branch and brand of Christianity today acknowledges some sense in which human beings are called to lives of priestly service.

What is a priest?   Most cultures and religions throughout history have understood priests (holy persons, shamans, witchdoctors, diviners, etc.) as mediators in some sense between God (the gods, the universe, oneness, spirits, etc.) and human beings. The priest is the person who stands at the intersection of the sacred and profane, the natural and the spiritual, relating the one to the other.

In the first instance, the priest stands before the god on behalf of people. She offers prayers and apologies, rituals and requests, supplications and sacrifices to please the god and ask for favor, provision, fertile crops, conquest over enemies, and safety from famine, tornado, and marauding warriors.

In the second instance, the priest stands before the people on behalf of the god. He delivers the words of the god and instructs them in the god's requirements; be it tithes or time, pilgrimage or blood sacrifice. If there is a human conduit of the god's blessing or wrath who can mumble holy words or concoct a holy potion as an agent of the divine it is the priest.

In this way, the priest is the broker between the human and divine. Every sacrament and ritual administered or presided over by the priest is either an offering to God or the gods on behalf of people or a representation of God or the gods back to the people.

This arrangement (or something analogous) is an almost universal characteristic of religion.

KEEP YOUR DISTANCE

This arrangement assumes a normative distance between God, sacred things, all manner of holiness and the everyday world where we live and hang out with friends, spend time with our families, go to work, go to school, and watch Fake News on

Comedy Central. We instinctively recognize this distance and are probably happy it maintained. Why?

We are sinful but God is immeasurably good and righteous. God seems inapproachable. Possibly even dangerous. Isn't this the primary logic of "reverence"? Best to tread carefully when it comes to holy matters for fear of offending our Creator, at best, and incurring the wrath of God at worst.

Consider Ancient Israel's religious system. The word for "holy" was nearly synonymous with "set apart."[5] In the Tabernacle or the Temple, the Holy Place was "set apart." "Set apart" even further was the place where God's presence and glory dwelt in the Holy of Holies - a place so unapproachable that only the High Priest could enter and only once a year.[6]

Part of the logic of the priesthood is to mediate this inapproachability.

If inapproachability is our baseline understanding of God, it makes sense to "set apart" priests to approach on our behalf. Like members of the bomb squad, they assume the risks associated with proximity to divinity ordinary folks would rather avoid. In turn, we ask them to bless us and tell us what God requires. They can even lay guilt trips and demand sacrifice as long as they also assure us of God's love and a place in heaven when we die.

---

[5] See entry for קֹדֶשׁ (holy) in Brown, F., Driver, S. R., & Briggs, C. A. (2000). *Enhanced Brown-Driver-Briggs Hebrew and English Lexicon*. Oak Harbor, WA: Logos Research Systems.
[6] On the Day of Atonement. See Leviticus 16.

Our typical construction of God and need for priests is built on the foundation of distance.

God is "Other" and does not belong to our world where we eat too much or drink too much, where we laugh at the wrong king of jokes, where we burp and fart.   God must be "set apart" from our laziness, our bad tempers, our everyday bigotry, our complicity with the evils of the world and our abounding wealth of shortcomings and failures that disqualify us from standing in the presence of God.

The gospel completely unravels this construction of a distant God.   Jesus reveals God is with us and for us in the middle of our messes.   Instead of insisting we become heavenly to know God, God inserts himself (in the incarnation of Jesus) right in the middle of our tears and joys, our successes and failures in order to be God to us, God with us, and God for us.

Jesus is the revelation that God gets his hands dirty in the mess of creation and most assuredly does *not* maintain a respectable distance from human beings on account of his holiness.   Jesus reveals that any need for sacrifice, any lack of forgiveness, and any shortcoming in character or behavior that might otherwise prevent us from relationship with God has been done away with effectively and forever.   In short, the mediation of Jesus as priest is final and eternal such that no further mediation is or ever will be necessary.

Any good reason God might have (or we might have) for keeping God and holy things at a distance has been done away with in Christ.   We don't need a mediator anymore.   In him, we have direct access to God.   The word, again, is parrhesia, and is also the foundation of the doctrine of Universal Priesthood.

As Colbert suggested, the image of God as a vengeful monkey must go.

LIVING IN THE LIGHT

If mediation is no longer required, what is the function of priests?

Here we've come full circle. You and I are supposed to do what the first Adam was supposed to do: Tend the garden. Be as Christ in this world. Work and create as those who bear the image of the Creator. Speak God's words of encourage ment, presence, and love to neighbor and enemy alike. Care for the poor and disenfranchised and share good news. Proclaim and revel in the presence of the present God. In this new day where sacrifice is no longer required, lift up life itself to God from whom we also receive life.

This is what it means to be a priest and a priestly people. You might express it in the words of the Baltimore Catechism cited by Stephen Colbert that we're here to know God, to love God, and to serve God.[7] If you prefer a Protestant spin you might like the Westminster Shorter Catechism, "The chief end of man is to glorify God and enjoy him forever."[8]

---

[7] A Catechism of Christian Doctrine, Prepared and Enjoined by Order of the Third Council of Baltimore, 1885, Part One, Lesson 1, Question and Answer 4.
[8] Westminster Shorter Catechism, 1647, Question and Answer 1.

A PRIEST'S WORK IS NEVER DONE

The priesthood of all believers is realized when the boundary between the sacred and profane, the natural world and God's world is breached (tear down that wall Mr. Gorbachev!).

This breach is no small theme in the Bible. At the death of Jesus, we're told that the curtain separating the Holy of Holies was torn in two.[9]   And not by human hands.

The message is clear. With Jesus, that day Habakkuk and Isaiah anticipated had arrived, when the glory of the LORD would go forth from the Temple and fill the whole earth as the waters fill the sea.[10]

This is also the message of angels appearing to shepherds at Christmastime.[11]   This is the message of Jesus praying, "Your kingdom come."[12]   This is the message spoken to the Samaritan woman that worship is not about choosing the right mountain or holy place it is about Spirit and truth.[13]   This is the message of Paul when he says, "Do everything in all that you do to the glory of God" whether you are slave or free.[14]   This is the message of the book of Revelation which envisions the New Jerusalem coming down from heaven to earth.[15]

The message is that God is not content with heaven being "up there" and earth "down here." He wants heaven to break its way into the "down here" starting with Jesus and continuing

---

[9] Matthew 27:51; Mark 15:38; Luke 23:45
[10] Habakkuk 2:14; Isaiah 11:9
[11] Luke 2:8-14
[12] Matthew 6:10; Luke 11:2
[13] John 4:19-24
[14] 1 Corinthians 10:31; Collosians 3:17
[15] Revelation 21:2

with you and me.   We, ourselves, are the site of new creation if we allow his transforming love and power to drive our existence such that our every moment, our every day is both gift and opportunity.

Jesus identified himself as the new Temple and names us as "living stones" included in that Temple by the Holy Spirit.[16]

Therefore, wherever we work, our job is in the Temple.   All work is priestly.   There is no longer mundane work to contrast with the sacred work.   All work is sacred.   All life is sacred. Our time, our laughter, our play, our projects, our floor sweeping, our car repairs, our relationships, and our conversations are "sown" in the life filled in-breaking kingdom of the Second Adam.

We're not forced to do anything.   If our moments and days are not sown in Christ we are free to have them.   It's just that in that case they are examples of spinning our wheels in the fear based and futile, distant-God, self-centered, fallen world that is decaying and passing away.   Plenty of human projects look like that.   But they certainly don't have to.   If we accept the gift, our lives and work have been lifted in Christ to something greater.

All of us are called to be priests.   All of us are charged to represent God's inexhaustible love to creation and lift up the best of creation to the glory of God.   Work is priestly.   While it is certainly possible to do bad work or to be a bad priest, work itself (as life itself) is priestly – an opportunity to embrace, lift up, and promote goodness to the glory – and don't miss it – the *enjoyment* of God.

---

[16] John 2:21; 1 Peter 2:5

This is unquestionably the ethos of *The Colbert Report*, a.k.a. the "Joy Machine."

On the one hand it is the forum where Father James Martin, Dan Savage, Deepak Chopra, Bill O'Reilly, Jimmy Carter, Willie Nelson, Pastor Jim Garlow, and many besides are given a voice and the dignity and respect (albeit sarcastically) to speak freely before God.   Nothing is off limits, nothing is off the table, contrary and conciliatory voices are given a forum to speak.

The Report is a conscious and intentional effort to seek joy and laughter, dispel fear, and speak truth under the guise of truthiness.   But doing so is work.   Having a vision to create laughter and produce joy in over a hundred and sixty shows per year takes effort.

Asked how he prepared for shows Colbert answered, "I read a lot of newspapers and watch a lot of news.   I've got twelve really good writers and then we chop wood all day long.   We show up exasperated or angry about something and we try to turn that into jokes six hours later."[17]

Call me crazy, but that is a calling.   And callings are sacred. Even priestly.

CALL ME CRAZY

I don't claim that Stephen Colbert puts on his suit in the morning like a cleric puts on his collar or understands himself

---

[17] *Meet the Press (TAKE TWO: msnbc.com)* with Tim Russert online exclusive aired October 21, 2007.   URL: http://www.nbcnews.com/video/meet-the-press/21400561#21400561

to be a priest.   I am not saying that Colbert or his writers are either mindful or in agreement with the brief theological sketch of Universal Priesthood offered above.   I am also not saying that anyone involved with the production of *The Colbert Report* believe that what they are producing is sacred.   If they did, the show would probably be tragically unfunny.

I *am* claiming that life itself is sacred.   That work itself is priestly.   And when we see it function well we should give a hearty, "Amen!"

Our culture of celebrity rarely gets its head around the fact that comedy is bigger than the comic just as art transcends the artist.   We may praise the artist and wonder at her ability to capture the profound and sublime, but it is the profound and sublime being lifted up rather than the artist herself.   The artist herself is not required to understand why or how her work is profound and sublime.   In fact, it is very likely that she will not comprehend it at all.   All she has to do is live out her calling.

This is priestly life.   We are all called to be artists, every one. Cornel West once said of a preacher (who probably would never have applied the word "artist" to himself), "He was first and foremost an artist.   And by "artist" I mean a Christian concerned about the art of living well and living lovingly."[18]

Priesthood can be expressed in a variety of ways.

Work and art as inherently worth doing is connected to our priesthood.   We create because we're made in the image of Creator God.   We build and dream up projects, we move

---

[18] Podcast, Smiley & West on PRI, featuring Tavis Smiley and Cornel West (discontinued)

from ideas to seeing those ideas manifested because we are priests and that is our calling.

In so far as our projects are based on a lust for power, greed, or selfishness they are akin to building Babel or Babylon.   Plenty of that goes on, but we're assured those buildings won't last.[19] On the other hand, when our projects are based on lifting up truth and bringing joy, dispelling fear through laughter – they are participation in the building of the New Jerusalem.

Musicians and moms, painters and plumbers, CEOs and comedians; all of us are all called to offer up our work.   As Colbert's guest NT Wright put it, made in God's image we are "angled mirrors" to reflect God's goodness onto creation, and reflect creation's praise back to God.[20]   As priests.   As priests who lift things up.

DUFUS

"What is the purpose of every day?" Colbert asked Rick Warren.

---

[19] 1 Corinthians 3:13, Revelation 18:2
[20] "This is what is meant by humans being made in God's image: not that we simply are like God in this or that respect, but that as angled mirrors we are called to sum up the praises of creation, on the one hand, and to rule as wise stewards over the world, on the other. This is the vocation known as the 'royal priesthood', kings and priests. (I have spelled all this out in much more detail in *After You Believe*.)" *Mind, Spirit, Soul and Body: All for One and One for All Reflections on Paul's Anthropology in his Complex Contexts,* Main Paper delivered at Society of Christian Philosophers: Regional Meeting, Fordham University, March 18, 2011.   URL: http://ntwrightpage.com/Wright_SCP_MindSpiritSoulBody.htm

Before he had a chance to respond Stephen continued, almost shouting, "Can I say what my purpose is? My purpose is to shout at people that I disagree with. Am I living my purpose, Rick?"

Warren took the chance to respond. Again, he might not have used the best words, but his point came across clearly:

"You know, when you be who God made you to be, that makes God smile. I used to think that God only smiles when we're doing, like, spiritual stuff: confessing, going to church, reading the Bible, things like that. But actually God gets enjoyment out of watching you be you.

"When my kids were little, I used to watch them sleep at night. And their little chests would rise and lower, rise and lower, and I got so much pleasure out of that, because I made them. I'm their daddy.

"And when you be who God made you to be, a dufus…. When you be *you*, God looks down and goes, "That's my boy!"

10.

Are You a Christian?

> "Let God be true and every man a liar."
>
> Romans 3:3[1]

CHRISTIAN

"Stephen Colbert isn't really a Christian, is he?" asked a friend. Several others asked the same thing when they learned I was writing about Stephen Colbert, Jesus, truth, and the gospel.

It's a bad question, of course, loaded with assumptions and tribal mentality. Moreover, it's not very Christian.

"I don't know..." I responded and let my voice trail off. Then I struck a pose of puzzlement and looked my friend in the eye, "Are *you* a Christian?" Oddly enough, when the question was directed at them they were offended.

---

[1] Romans 3:3, author's translation

Seeking to identify celebrities as "in" or "out" with respect to God and faith is silly. Doing so typically involves invoking a litmus test consisting of invented criteria that has more to do with brand identification than Jesus or the gospel.

In the late 1980s, pockets of the American Evangelical Christian community celebrated pop band U2 as "Christian." In the early 1990s, U2's artistic statement changed. The band assumed glitzy rockstar personas, simultaneously embracing and critiquing pop culture. Outward appearances were enough for some to claim the band had "lost their faith." In 2010, when U2 put out a fresh batch of songs proclaiming faith and reliance on God, some of the same people hailed them as "Christian" again.

Jesus words about "judging not" offer the better part of wisdom. Authentic artistic voices are stifled when armchair observers sit in judgment or "haters" fill the comments section of web pages with toxicity.

Deciding whether Justin Bieber, Katy Perry, Mumford and Sons, or Stephen Colbert are "faith-filled" is a task no one is called to. We lack the criteria and the capacity for such judgments.

Johnny Cash once wrote, "I love songs about horses, railroads, land, Judgment Day, family, hard times, whiskey, courtship, marriage, adultery, separation, murder, war, prison, rambling, damnation, home, salvation, death, pride, humor, piety, rebellion, patriotism, larceny, determination, tragedy, rowdiness, heartbreak and love. And Mother. And God."[2]

---

[2] *American Recordings II: Unchained,* 1996, Johnny Cash, American / Warner Bros, album liner notes.

Cash's murder ballads and songs about cheating are not grounds to conclude that he is a murderer or an endorser of infidelity.   Outside of Cash's art, when he got busted for drug possession it was no one's job to decide whether he still loved God or if God still loved him.   If you Johnny Cash personally…   You might be qualified to weigh in with some advice.   But judging the state of a person's heart through the media or television is reckless.

Listening, engaging, and even judging what Cash's art says about God, humanity, sin, salvation, truth, wonder, and beauty…   That's completely legitimate.   So is paying attention to what might emerge with respect to these topics in spite of the artists.   Whether or not Stephen Colbert is a Christian is beside the point.

Are *you* a Christian?

WHO IS THIS MAN THAT WE SHOULD BE MINDFUL OF HIM?

Stephen Colbert is the youngest of eleven children (the first hint that he grew up in a Catholic home).   He was raised in Charleston, South Carolina.   His father, James, was a doctor on staff at the Medical School of South Carolina.   His mother, Lorna, once aspired to be in theatre but through a set of strange circumstances (literally involving a rare tropical disease and falling in love)[3] she happily embraced being a mother and homemaker.

---

[3] *The Paul Mecurio Show* (#26) interview with Stephen Colbert on August 12, 2013.   Podcast URL:

The Colbert household was church-going and devout. Colbert's mother and father engaged their religious beliefs. They celebrated Christian holidays, the young Colbert went to religious schools and served eleven straight years as an altar boy from age 7.

As an altar boy, Colbert sang and attended Sunday masses but also served at weddings and funerals. Colbert said he was drawn to the red and black cassocks that "made you look like a mini-priest" but usually had to settle for the simple, white, monk-like robes.[4]

The Colbert household was a close, love infused environment. Thanks to his mother's love of theatre, all manner of acting and performance was encouraged. Laughter and comedy was embraced. Colbert, the youngest, has fond memories of being allowed to stay up late whenever a comedian was featured on *The Tonight Show Starring Johnny Carson*.[5]

On September 11, 1974, tragedy struck.

Colbert's father James and his two older brothers Peter and Paul were killed in a plane crash in North Carolina. The two boys were traveling with their father to enroll in school in Connecticut. Stephen was ten years old when his father and the two siblings nearest his own age passed away.

---

http://sideshownetwork.tv/podcastsEpisode.cfm?podcastid=68&episodeID=2659

[4] "Exclusive Interview: Rev. Sir Dr. Stephen T. Colbert, D.F.A." by DB Ferguson, posted on fan site www.nofactzone.net May 20, 2011.   URL: http://www.nofactzone.net/2011/05/21/exclusive-interview-rev-sir-dr-stephen-t-colbert-d-f-a/

[5] *The Paul Mecurio Show* (#26) interview with Stephen Colbert on August 12, 2013.   Podcast URL: http://sideshownetwork.tv/podcastsEpisode.cfm?podcastid=68&episodeID=2659

Obviously, this event was profoundly formative for Stephen Colbert. It continues to be a focal point of interviews and serious out-of-character discussions with the comic.

"If that tragedy hadn't happened," asked friend and fellow comedian Paul Mecurio, "Do you think you'd be doing what you're doing today?"

"I'd be a totally different person," Colbert responded.[6]

In many ways, the tragedy left the youngest Colbert as an only child. His nearest living sibling was nine and a half years his senior. Not surprisingly, his mother went through a period of great grief and was the opposite of smothering.

"It was like, 'You're alive, you're fine,'" Colbert quipped.[7]

In that same period of time the Colbert family moved to a different part of Charleston and Stephen went through a period of social isolation. Colbert began to read voraciously. He was drawn to the fantasy worlds of *Dungeons and Dragons* and especially Tolkien's "Middle Earth." He read *The Lord of the Rings* and *The Hobbit* repeatedly.

Colbert never outgrew his fantasy fandom. *The Colbert Report* has been a platform for "Hobbit Week," trivia showdowns with other Tolkien know-it-alls (Colbert always wins), and Colbert even got himself a cameo appearance in Peter Jackson's 2013 film *The Desolation of Smaug.*[8]

---

[6] Ibid.

[7] Ibid.

[8] Hobbit Week was episodes 1123-1126, aired on December 3-6, 2012. Stephen Colbert appeared as a Lake-town spy in *The Desolation of*

In high school, Colbert hardly applied himself but his ample reading habits were enough to carry him through graduation and into Harper-Sydney College in Virginia. In Virginia, philosophy was Colbert's main area of study until he transferred after two years to Northwestern University in Chicago to major in theatre. His dabbling in theatre at Harper-Sydney revealed to him that of all his pursuits, it was acting he found himself engaging most passionately.

In either school, however, college was not a happy time for Stephen Colbert. It was eight years after the loss of his father and brothers, but that was when the grief hit him the hardest.

"For years I thought that that was my secret name," he explained to Oprah, "the loss of my father and brothers."[9]

Not unrelated, his faith was also in crisis.

"The minute I went to college, I didn't believe in God. The minute I had an opportunity to sort of be out from under the constant exposure to my faith, I accepted the opportunity to not believe. And I was very convinced of my atheism for a long time, and I was very depressed about it. I wanted very much to believe... I wanted the idea that I would see my father and my brothers again, and it was heartbreaking to think that that wouldn't happen. The fool says in his heart that there is no God, and I was sad to be that fool. I would rather have been a fool for God, but I was so convinced that believing in God was

---

Smaug (2013) directed by Peter Jackson, Newline Cinema, MGM, Wingnut Films.

[9] *Oprah's Next Chapter:* "Will the Real Stephen Colbert Please Stand Up?" Interview with Oprah, aired September 30, 2012. URL: http://www.oprah.com/own-oprahs-next-chapter/Oprah-Meets-the-Real-Stephen-Colbert-Video

foolish. There were five years maybe when I couldn't think of why to get up. That wasn't good."[10]

Colbert's unhappiness affected his pursuit of vocation.   He never intended to be a comedian.   He was not pursuing comedic acting.   He intended to be a serious actor who wore black and was eager to share his misery.[11]   Ironically, the atheist Colbert even sported an artsy Jesus beard.

"I didn't want to play Hamlet, I wanted to be Hamlet."[12]

While Colbert had done some improv as a student at Northwestern, he'd been taught to look down his nose at the low brow comedy of Chicago's Second City.[13]   After graduation, however, he was in need of work.   Fearing the rejection that would come with seeking acting gigs he took a job at Second City answering phones.

As an employee of Second City, Colbert took advantage of the free classes the company offered which started to open his mind about comedic acting.   During this period, Colbert experienced two epiphanies that would alter his course profoundly.   If you prefer, he was converted.   Twice!   And in two different ways, by two very different sets of evangelists.

---

[10] "Stephen Colbert Web Exclusive" in *Parade* online, September 4, 2007, from interview with James Kaplan.   URL: http://parade.condenast.com/50118/parade/stephen-colbert-web-exclusive/
[11] "Stephen Colbert" by Nathan Rabin, AV Club Interview, January 25, 2006. URL: http://www.avclub.com/article/stephen-colbert-13970
[12] "The Man in the Irony Mask" by Seth Mnookin. October, 2007. Vanity Fair, URL: http://www.vanityfair.com/culture/features/2007/10/colbert200710
[13] "How Many Stephen Colbert's Are There?" by Charles McGrath in *The New York Times Magazine* published January 4, 2012.   URL: http://www.nytimes.com/2012/01/08/magazine/stephen-colbert.html?ref=magazine&_r=0

One set of evangelists were the Gideons handing out Bibles on the streets of Chicago. The others were irreverent comedians Paul Dinello and Amy Sedaris.

NEW LIFE

On a cold winter day in Chicago Stephen Colbert was handed a Bible. Turning to Matthew 5 he began to read the Sermon on the Mount.

"I didn't read it. It spoke to me."[14]   He was confronted with the words of Jesus, "Do not be worried about your life... Look at the birds of the air, that they do not sow, nor reap nor gather into barns, yet your heavenly Father feeds them. Are you not worth much more than they? And who of you by being worried can add a single hour to his life?"[15]

It was a pivotal encounter for Colbert.

"The desire to believe always was there. The fact that thread was never cut was helpful."[16]   Letting faith back into his life was letting joy back in, joy that springs up even in the midst of death. It didn't hurt that this was precisely what his mother had modeled.

---

[14] "The Subversive Joy of Stephen Colbert" by Neil Straus, September 17, 2009, *Rolling Stone Magazine*, URL: http://www.rollingstone.com/movies/news/the-subversive-joy-of-stephen-colbert-20090917#ixzz37eQ39YfD

[15] Matthew 6:25-26, *New American Standard Bible: 1995 update*. (1995). LaHabra, CA: The Lockman Foundation.

[16] "Stephen Colbert Web Exclusive" in *Parade* online, September 4, 2007, from interview with James Kaplan. URL: http://parade.condenast.com/50118/parade/stephen-colbert-web-exclusive/

"She raised me after her husband and two of her boys died – and she did a great job, and her faith played a great role in that. She's a loving, joyful, not-bitter woman and, boy, that's a great example to have in your life. It makes your travails seem pretty simple in respect."[17]

Faith in a suffering Messiah and the example of his mother enabled Colbert to cope with his own suffering, but also to accept it as a gift.   An earlier quote deserves its larger context here.

Stephen elucidated, "There's a common explanation that profound sadness leads to someone's becoming a comedian, but I'm not sure that's a proven equation in my case...   I'm not bitter about what happened to me as a child, and my mother was instrumental in keeping me from being so... She taught me to be grateful for my life regardless of what that entailed, and that's directly related to the image of Christ on the cross and the example of sacrifice that he gave us. What she taught me is that the deliverance God offers you from pain is not no pain — it's that the pain is actually a gift. What's the option? God doesn't really give you another choice."[18]

Elsewhere Colbert added, "Not to get too deep here, but the most valuable thing I can think of is to be grateful for suffering. That is a sublime feeling, and completely inexplicable and illogical, but no one doesn't suffer. So the

[17] "The Subversive Joy of Stephen Colbert" by Neil Straus, September 17, 2009, *Rolling Stone Magazine*, URL: http://www.rollingstone.com/movies/news/the-subversive-joy-of-stephen-colbert-20090917#ixzz37eQ39YfD
[18] "How Many Stephen Colbert's Are There?" by Charles McGrath in *The New York Times Magazine* published January 4, 2012.   URL: http://www.nytimes.com/2012/01/08/magazine/stephen-colbert.html?ref=magazine&_r=0

degree to which you can be aware of your own humanity is the degree to which you can accept, with open eyes, your suffering. To be grateful for your suffering is to be grateful for your humanity, because what else are you going to do? Say, "No, thanks"? It's there. "Smile and accept," said Mother Teresa. And she was talking to people who had it rough."[19]

ANOTHER CONVERSION

If the Gideons helped facilitate a fresh wind of life in the recently graduated and maturing Stephen Colbert, another spark of renewal was fanned into flame by his Second City compatriots Amy Sedaris and Paul Dinello.

When Colbert started at Second City he took himself rather seriously. Dinello and Sedaris continually sought to disabuse Colbert of his self-importance and cajole him into embracing the silly and ridiculous.

"He showed up with really high hair and an actor's attitude," said Dinello. "[Sedaris and I] were more like clowns. We tried to corrupt him."[20]

Not wanting to be thought a fool and protecting his ego were part of Colbert's defenses. Eventually they were brought down. Colbert recalled the exact moment it happened, waiting in the wings of the "E.T.C. stage" of Second City in 1993.

---

[19] "The Man in the Irony Mask" by Seth Mnookin. October, 2007. *Vanity Fair.* URL:
http://www.vanityfair.com/culture/features/2007/10/colbert200710
[20] Ibid.

Colbert was backstage with colleague Dave Razowsky. The duo were waiting their turn to go on for a sketch. In the spotlight was Jenna Jolovitz who was performing a tried, tested, and true joke – not a piece of high art but a reliable bit.

The spoof was that the actor would take up the persona of a folk singer and declare her intention to perform a song for the whales. She would proceed to build up anticipation, tune imaginary guitar strings, feign profound empathy, until she would finally burst out with "bhwooooaaa, ooomm, oooeee" type whale sounds in the *Finding Nemo* style of Ellen DeGeneres.

Colbert said about the formula, "It's not a great joke but it never fails... it always kills... It's all about building up audience expectations and then a brief punch."[21]

Colbert and Razowsky were waiting their turn while Jolovitz performed. When she started the song, they realized something had gone wrong. She was singing in her best whale voice but the audience was flat. No response. No laughter. Colbert and Razowsky were bewildered and looked at each other mystified until Jolovitz spurted on stage, "Oh... I forgot to tell you... It's a song for whales!"[22]

A complete bomb.

Colbert burst into gales of laughter along with Razowsky. The two started hugging each other giggling and literally fell to the ground in joy kicking their legs and howling with laughter. Seeing their spasming legs on the side of the stage, Jolovitz

---

[21] *A.D.D. Comedy Podcast with Dave Razowsky and Ian Foley*, November 20, 2012, interview with Stephen Colbert
[22] Ibid.

could do nothing else but join in the uncontrollable laughter before a mystified audience. The joy was not in their fellow comedian's suffering, their joy was in identification with her suffering.[23]

"In that moment [I realized] I will do this... I *must* do this for a living. Because if there can be this much joy at a moment of this much agony and this much failure... Well there is something very healthy about that. And I can clearly and without hesitancy say that is when I decided to become a comedian."[24]

Sedaris and Dinello's gospel invitation for Stephen Colbert to get over himself finally hit its mark. Giving up credibility and letting go of respectability can be taught, but ultimately it needs to be *caught* – very much like faith itself.

"Something burst that night, and I finally let go of the pretension of not wanting to be a fool."[25]

SURRENDER

Surrender is essential for embracing comedy as vocation. Perhaps, surrender is at the heart of every artistic vocation. Surrender is certainly at the heart of the gospel.

Faith in Jesus is a de-centering endeavor. The phrases "Do not worry" and "Do not be afraid" are a profound summons.

---

[23] Ibid.
[24] Ibid.
[25] "Stephen Colbert: If You are Laughing, You Can't Be Afraid" by James Kaplan, Parade Magazine, 2007. URL: http://entertainment.msn.com/news/article.aspx?news=279074

They are not words of assurance saying 'bad things won't happen' or 'risks are not real.' They are the invitation to abandon control over existence and give it up to God. As anyone who has experienced loss or tragedy can attest, being in control of our own lives is an illusion anyway.

At the heart of the Christian gospel is the call to give up on worth as self-generated or self-achieved and accept worth and love as pure gift from God in Christ. We are invited to release our grasp of the kingdoms we build and embrace God's kingdom which is always gift.

Give up credibility today.

As Paul put it, "I have been crucified with Christ."[26]

Jesus said the same, "If anyone would come after me, let them deny themselves, take up their cross, and follow me."[27]

In doing so, we don't just count ourselves dead. We count ourselves dead *in Christ*. We send our credibility, respectability, pomp, and pride to *his* cross because *his* death is the place out of which resurrection is birthed.

The phrase "in Christ" is used repeatedly in the New Testament. This is precisely the idea invoked. All attempts at achieving meaning and significance on our own go to the cross. What is left is the gift of God – the resurrection life of Jesus. Our lives have meaning precisely because they are participation in Christ's eternal life.

---

[26] Galatians 2:20, *The New International Version*. (2011). Grand Rapids, MI: Zondervan.
[27] Matthew 16:24, author's translation.

Here, inside that life, there is nothing to fear because Christ has nothing to fear.

"As he is, so are we in this world."[28]

There is no anxiety concerning condemnation, no standard of performance to fall short of, no respectability to protect. We have freedom to be and speak and live in the presence of God because our life is in Christ.

Only in this way can we accept life, suffering, and even tragic suffering as gift. If our lives are "in Christ" then our sufferings are indeed "participation in his suffering" which result in life. Why? The Christian gospel is not about avoiding death, it's the message that the deaths and the crosses we face do not have the last word but God vindicates cross bearers and sufferers with resurrection life.

We can draw the analogy with comedy.

"If you cling to your life, you will lose it, but if you give up your life for me, you will find it."[29]

If your primary concern is to protect your dignity, you might realize your goal, but you certainly won't be funny. Getting over yourself, telling your secrets, abandoning your credibility, rejecting fear, allowing the truth to set you free, receiving love and the free speech of parrhesia, accepting what comes, and embracing it all as gift...

These are what the gospel is all about. And these are what make for great comedy and great comics.

---

[28] 1 John 4:17
[29] Tyndale House Publishers. (2007). *Holy Bible: New Living Translation* (3rd ed., Mt 10:39). Carol Stream, IL: Tyndale House Publishers.

I AM VERY HARD TO EMBARRASS

For Stephen Colbert, it is easy to recognize his abandonment of self-importance as central to his comedic project in *The Colbert Report*. If Colbert weren't able to "be the fool" the show could not exist. His books, silly skits, songs with guests, public stunts, and unrelenting commitment to an idiotic persona all evidence he is unfettered by concern of appearing foolish.

A perfect example came in a segment of *The Colbert Report* in 2007 called "For Your Editing Pleasure." Colbert complained about politicians being warned to avoid his show because "he gets that last edit." Mockingly insisting that such concerns were for naught, Colbert subjected himself to an interview with PBS's Gwen Ifill which he invited anyone and everyone to edit as they saw fit.

In the interview, Colbert deliberately and slowly used obvious key words that could be re-cut to construe scandalous statements. To drive the point home, Ifill asked Colbert to read a list of words (making sure the paper was off camera) which included "shaven," "drunken," "kill all," "every American's duty," and more. The self-confident character of Stephen Colbert then challenged the "wizards" of editing "out there" to do their worst. He couldn't possibly be misinterpreted.

Heaps of viewers with video editing savvy responded to the challenge. Entries can still be watched on *The Colbert Report's* Comedy Central website. Warning: Not for the sensitive or easily offended! As Colbert once responded when asked if he would run for office, "I have said terrible things with a straight face on camera."[30]

"I think all the time about something my mother said to me many times as a child: "In the light of eternity, what does this matter?" In that regard, I'm very hard to embarrass. I really don't mind making a fool of myself, because I have some sense of who I am beyond this fool – I hope... I don't mind looking like an idiot or being ugly. That helps me a lot, and I definitely get that from my mom. "None of this matters" is what I was taught over and over again."[31]

ARE YOU RELIGIOUS TOMORROW?

The willingness to surrender and the freedom to be a fool is a comedic but also a gospel orientation. Stephen Colbert and the staff of the *The Colbert Report* might not characterize their calling in this way, but the ethos is clearly embodied.

Colbert has admitted that his faith matters to him deeply while at times it feels distant or like going through the motions.[32] He has served as a Sunday School teacher for seven year olds preparing for their first communion.[33] He has confessed

---

[30] On *Meet the Press* with David Gregory on NBC, published October 14, 2012. URL:
http://www.nbcnews.com/video/meet-the-press/49407301
[31] "The Subversive Joy of Stephen Colbert" by Neil Straus, September 17, 2009, *Rolling Stone Magazine*, URL:
http://www.rollingstone.com/movies/news/the-subversive-joy-of-steph en-colbert-20090917#ixzz37eQ39YfD
[32] *A.D.D. Comedy Podcast with Dave Razowsky and Ian Foley*, November 20, 2012, interview with Stephen Colbert
[33] "The Subversive Joy of Stephen Colbert" by Neil Straus, September 17, 2009, Rolling Stone Magazine, URL:

shortcomings in terms of fervently sticking to Catholic dogma and in practicing what he preaches.   He has also affirmed questioning the Church as a legitimate part of belonging to the Church.

Thankfully, Stephen Colbert's precise spiritual location at any given moment is beside the point.   Whether he is in a place of doubt or deep faith, deviation or devotion, Colbert's vocation is to drive forward the fearless freedom of the Joy Machine. His job is not to get things "right" theologically, it is to set the stage for truth to shine.   Freedom to be a fool is freedom to be wrong, freedom to be confused, freedom to seek, and freedom to laugh.

There is a certain level of surrender, on the one hand, and acceptance on the other that is required for both gospel and comedy.   You don't have to be perfect to enjoy the gift, you just have to embrace it and let it operate.   Producing 160 shows a year does not leave time for naval gazing.

"Doing this many shows…   There is very little threshold for your emotions being more important than… the idea of the show."[34]

Speaking about the difficulty of getting shows done Stephen spoke of surrender, "The taskmaster that 'it must be done' lets you surrender your preciousness about things… Which is

http://www.rollingstone.com/movies/news/the-subversive-joy-of-stephen-colbert-20090917#ixzz37eQ39YfD

[34] *A.D.D. Comedy Podcast with Dave Razowsky and Ian Foley*, November 20, 2012, interview with Stephen Colbert

hubris! It's not going to be *that* much better if you spend another 30 minutes on it. *Show* the people!"[35]

"You have to look at the demand of the show as a gift. I have an idea today, or even a subject that interests me even if I don't have the idea and we have a great team of people and tonight we can talk about it. That's a gift."[36]

The alternative, for Colbert, is when the regularity of the show feels like a blade coming at him.

"Sometimes I feel like I do the show "head down." That's how I describe it. I'm doing the show "head down" because I'm afraid it's going to lop me off."[37]

If a comic is too careful, they are too self-conscious. When a comic is too self-conscious, the comedy is neither funny nor truthful. Colbert cautions that fear and over-sensitivity are stifling.

"Now we're in the big leagues. If it's not good tonight, or if tonight I don't say what I mean or if I don't express in a unique way or at least in a way unique to this show then the blade is going to chop my head off. You can't think that way. You have to just do the show."[38]

When Rolling Stone interviewed Stephen Colbert in his office in 2009 he had two pieces of paper taped to his computer. One said, 'Joy is the most infallible sign of the presence of God.'

---

[35] Ibid.

[36] Ibid.

[37] Ibid.

[38] Ibid.

Colbert said, "I call the show 'The Joy Machine,' because if you can do it with joy, even in the simplest show, then it's 'The Joy Machine' as opposed to 'The Machine.' Considering the speed at which we do it, we'll get caught in the gears really quickly unless we also approach it with joy."[39]

The other piece of paper simply says, 'Work.'

"I have 'work' here and 'joy' over there, and I try to put the two together somehow."

FOOLS

Surrender and acceptance are how Stephen Colbert can reach beyond himself, dispensing with concerns about his own inadequacies (real or imagined), insecurities, or social apprehensions to let the truth roll on. He can make space at the table for a myriad of voices including New Ager Deepak Chopra, Buddhist Lama Surya Das, atheist Richard Dawkins, agnostic Bart Ehrman, Rabbi Ron Fish, Hindu Uma Mysorekar, as well as "closer to home" types like Jesuit Father James Martin.

Colbert mockingly "took to task" American nuns for paying too much attention to the poor and not enough attention to forbidding contraceptives. In doing so, he took the role of the buffoon to make room for their authentic voice.

---

[39] "The Subversive Joy of Stephen Colbert" by Neil Straus, September 17, 2009, *Rolling Stone Magazine*, URL:
http://www.rollingstone.com/movies/news/the-subversive-joy-of-steph
en-colbert-20090917#ixzz37eQ39YfD

Colbert expressed disapproval toward Pope Francis' cautionary statements about unhampered capitalism. In doing so, he exposed the gap between the theoretical alignment of Christians with Jesus and actual adherence to his words and teachings.

For evangelicals, one of Stephen Colbert's favorite questions is a one-two punch set up. He asks something like, "Do you believe the Bible is inerrant?" When the guest answers affirmatively Colbert quips, "Then you believe we should stone gay people! It says it right there in Leviticus that we should stone gay people."[40]

The joke is not there to mock religious belief. On the contrary, it is an opportunity for guests to authentically express their character and faith and how they grapple with inherited tradition and sources of religious authority.

Colbert is the fool precisely so that they can be genuine.

When Stephen put that question to Rick Warren in the same interview discussed last chapter Warren rolled his eyes and asked despairingly, "Who are your writers?"

Colbert answered aggressively, "Tonight I only have one, the inerrant word of God!"[41]

Christian sociologist, activist, and actor Tony Campolo replied to the same question, "Jesus upped the ante of moral action to 'Love your neighbor as yourself.'"[42]

---

[40] Stephen Colbert posed this question on *The Colbert Report* to David Plotz on March 31, 2009; Bishop Gene Robinson on April 26, 2013; Tony Campolo on February 4, 2008; and Rick Warren on January 28, 2008.
[41] Episode 344, aired January 28, 2008

AFFECTED

"You are devoutly religious," suggested Paul Mecurio when he sat down with Stephen Colbert.[43]

Mecurio was a co-writer with Colbert in the early days of *The Daily Show with John Stewart*. He was genuinely enthusiastic talking about the joys of comedy in general and the craft of Stephen Colbert in particular.

Colbert shirked at the characterization, "Ehhhh…"

The tone of his voice made it clear to listeners that he was uncomfortable being pigeon holed.

"Comparatively… to a lot of the people I know in comedy I'm 'devoutly religious'… but that doesn't mean a lot."

Pressed a little harder he admitted, "I happen to be profoundly affected by the story of Jesus. I can no more remove that from me than you can the marble from the shape of a statue. That is just who I am."[44]

---

[42] Episode 348, aired February 4, 2008

[43] *The Paul Mecurio Show* (#26) interview with Stephen Colbert on August 12, 2013. Podcast URL: http://sideshownetwork.tv/podcastsEpisode.cfm?podcastid=68&episo deID=2659

[44] Colbert acknowledged he was paraphrasing Robert Bolt (*A Man For All Seasons*).

11.

We're All Gonna Die

"Whoever wants to be my disciple must deny themselves and take up their cross and follow me.   For whoever wants to save their life will lose it, but whoever loses their life for me will find it."

Luke 16:24-25[1]

WE'RE ALL GONNA DIE

The meaning of life is learning how to die.

At least, that's the argument of "friend of the show" and public intellectual Cornel West.   In developing this insight West cites Plato's argument that philosophy is a preparation for death and Montaigne who flat out declared, "To philosophize is to learn how die."

"You can't talk about truth," said West, "Without talking about learning how to die."[2]

---

[1] Matthew 16:24-25, *The New International Version*. (2011). Grand Rapids, MI: Zondervan.

Such a perspective could hardly be called popular. West's claims about truth and the meaning of life strikingly out of alignment with the dominant cultural narrative. In the not-so-philosophical everyday world where most of us live and breathe we do not typically think of our purpose in terms of preparation for death. In fact, death is something we would prefer to think about as little as possible. Our obsession is the opposite. We strive for health, beauty, looking younger, feeling fitter, eradicating wrinkles, and tucking tummies. Our practices indicate a belief that the slow march from womb to tomb is a march in the wrong direction - a cruel imposition of fate (or God, or sin).

But time waits for no one. You might get out of paying taxes, but unless your name is Enoch, Elijah, or possibly the Blessed Mother you won't get out of dying.[3] Even Jesus had to go through death to arrive at resurrection life. Having taken that path, moreover, he bid everyone else to follow him. As Hank Williams crooned poetically, "No matter how I struggle and strive, I'll never get out of this world alive."[4]

Or as Cornel West is fond of saying, "You will one day be the culinary delight of terrestrial worms."[5]

---

[2] *Examined Life* (2008), a documentary directed by Astra Taylor, Zeitgeist Films, featuring Cornel West waxing eloquent in a cab ride through New York City.

[3] Cf. Genesis 5:24, 2 Kings 2:11

[4] *I'll Never Get Out Of This World Alive,* 1952, written by Hank Williams and Fred Rose. Ironically, this was the last single released while Hank Williams was still living (it reached #1).

[5] For example, Episode 626, aired October 26, 2009.

THE GOOD LIFE

We all know this. Yet this knowledge rarely leads us to confront death or attempt to understand it. It's easier to assume that our purpose is to run against the stream of our eventual demise and squeeze out of our temporal reality as much pleasure as we can.

If life is like a short ride at an amusement park – the purpose (it would seem) is to clamor for the best seat, the best view, or whatever else we can do to enjoy and extend the ride as much as possible. To say that the better part of the ride is acknowledging its shortness and preparing to get off seems profoundly counter cultural if not absurd.

Avoiding death is a more persuasive motivation for everyday living than embracing death or preparing for it.   Our constructions of the good life (religious, social, etc.) reflect this. Death denying visions of human flourishing are more attractive than those that acknowledge mortality.

Politicians, religions, and corporations know this all too well. Those who would vie for our attention, seek our allegiance, or gain some modicum of control over us consciously and unconsciously seek to influence our voting patterns, behaviors, and purchasing habits by appealing to our passion for an imagined death-denying good life.

Consider a hypothetical coffee company. To push their product they attempt to associate it with the consumer's vision of the good life – a real or ideal conception of life lived to the fullest.

An effective TV commercial might feature a beautiful and spacious cabin deep in the woods. Outside the window large snowflakes are falling like in a Christmas special. Soft, enchanting music plays in the background. The camera brings us inside where we see loved ones sharing smiles of comfort and joy beside a fire as they nestle coffee mugs in hand.

The company portrays the good life, associates their product with that life, and we consume it in pursuit of the life portrayed. This is a pretty basic formula for consumerism. Sometimes it is a little more abstract.

Perhaps the portrayal of the good life is a display of cleverness, artsiness, or even cynicism that is supposed to cull desire. But death is rarely present. There is no urn on the mantelpiece in the craftsman cottage.

If death does show up in advertising it is with products like diets, gym memberships, or plastic surgery where the message is, "Death is coming. Quick!   Consume this and live forever."

This is not entirely bad. Consumeristic drive is spawned by wants but also needs. Our desire for life motivates us to buy eggs and bread as much as it motivates us to buy sports cars or diamonds. Desiring and pursuing robust life is good and appropriate. Even Jesus declared, "I have come that they might have life and have it to the full!"[6]

There are two easy and obvious ways our healthy appetite for living can be perverted (in the original sense of being bent, twisted from the original aim).

---

[6] John 10:10, *The New International Version*. (2011). Grand Rapids, MI: Zondervan.

First, is if the conception of the good life we develop (or the conception that is fed to us) is neither good nor living.   If our conception of the good life is self-centered or depends on the exploitation of others it is neither good nor alive in the sense that God is good and the author of life.

Our conception of the good life is distorted if it does not acknowledge finitude – if it does not accept and embrace the reality of death, temporality, and contingency.   Stuff doesn't last!   If your conception of the highest good is wrapped up in something that won't last it will lead you to despair or denial.

Despair is the more rational of the two.   In light of the recognition that all things living come to death, despair is neither stupid nor illogical.   It is the acknowledgment of death but an acknowledgment that is devoid of hope.   Despair can lead to hopelessness or suicide.

Denial is less honest than despair, but it is also less tragic.   In this sense, we might consider it a happy that our culture prefers denial to despair.

Denial of death is the engine that drives our culture's construction and maintenance of idols.   Idols of wealth, strength, beauty, youth, and pleasure.

The pursuit of happiness is often equated to the pursuit of places where we can live as though death does not exist. Happiness, in this paradigm, is the temporary suspension of apprehending death.   This sense of "happiness" is different and inferior to joy.

Happiness is pleasure "in the moment" but as a result it is necessarily temporary and most often fleeting.   Joy, on the other hand, endures because it acknowledges death. Joy takes account of present pleasures but also past and future pain, holding them acceptingly in hope. As Stephen Colbert observed, "Joy can be hard. Joy is not the same thing as happiness… Happiness is overrated."[7]

Our fragile cultural idols (wealth, strength, beauty, youth, pleasure) motivate us to live for the purpose of pursuing happiness as opposed to learning how to die. In what sense are they fragile? Precisely because they are unable to outlast or triumph over death.

Death remains the dominant reality to be grappled with. Death is all around us. Our pets die, our cousins die, our firewood was alive but now is dead. Every bite of food we take that gives us nourishment is predicated on death. Some plant or animal has to die if we are to live.

We're all going to die.

But this is terrifying. So we stubbornly persist in envisioning a good life where death is absent. Meanwhile, the primary mechanism for protecting our fragile façade is fear. Fear becomes the very ethos of a death denying culture. If our best vision of life is wrapped up in our perceived freedoms, our wealth, our comfort and security, our isolation and separation from the sorrows of the world – we have every reason to be terrified.

---

[7] *Oprah's Next Chapter: Will the Real Stephen Colbert Please Stand Up?* Interview with Oprah, aired September 30, 2012. URL: http://www.oprah.com/own-oprahs-next-chapter/Oprah-Meets-the-Real-Stephen-Colbert-Video

Fear is always the fear of death.   In this sense it is the shadow side of our desire for life. Fear is protective and defensive in nature.   The more death denying our construction of the good life, the larger and more powerful fear will loom.

This is not to say fear is never appropriate.   Fear of getting too close to the ledge while visiting the Grand Canyon or driving when conditions are unsafe is protective and preservative.   At its root it is still the fear of death.   Fear of failure, fear of embarrassment, fear of spiders… All of these are connected with our conception of the good life we wish to protect.   And the opposite of life is death.   Even in the most minute sense possible, fear is always the fear of death.

Our conception of the good life might be deplorable.   We may think "happiness" is pursuing our own happiness at the expense of others.

Our fears may be completely irrational.   Many of the things we fear are imagined and don't correspond to actual threats or danger to our well-being.

Whatever else is true, the abundance of fear in our world and in our culture is evidence that we are not adequately prepared for death.   Back to Cornel West's point, you can't talk about truth without talking about learning to die.

BE AFRAID

But we don't!   We do not talk about learning how to die or preparing ourselves for death or anything of the sort.   The result?   Fear is rampant. As long as we ignore death as a certainty to prepare for and are willing to go to great lengths to avoid facing it, we cultivate fertile ground for the production of fear and facilitate its spread.

Fear grips our minds and enslaves us with ever increasing anxiety and multiplying fear.   It should terrify you just thinking about it!   Not only that, fear can be wielded as a powerful tool for tyranny, control, and manipulation.   It is no surprise, then, that fear is nothing short of currency in our death denying world.

We're   afraid   of   terrorists,   nuclear   war,   immigrants, unemployment, and our political opponents.   We're afraid of diseases, afraid of neighbors, afraid of police, afraid of the roads, afraid of weather, and afraid of people who do not look like us or talk like us or act like us.   Fear has the power to drive the world.   It can compel votes, it can be used to get children to   behave,   it   can   be   employed   by   religious   groups   to manipulate   whole   communities   with   the   fear   of   hell, condemnation, and social ostracization.

Fear is more likely to render us powerless than empower us toward goodness of any kind – especially if the root of our fear is an inability to accept the reality of death and suffering.   To seek a deep joy that acknowledges both is far better than seeking a shallow happiness that insists on uninterrupted pleasure.   Ironically,   the   fears   invoked   to   protect   our happiness are more likely to rob us of it then protect us from the object of our fear.

Once upon a time, Franklin D. Roosevelt captured the imagination of Americans by exposing precisely this irony; "The only thing we have to fear is fear itself."[8]

BE AFRAID, BE VERY AFRAID

Fear is used to enslave, subjugate, and manipulate. Take terrorism, for example. Terrorists get their name for acting in a way that stirs up terror – pure unadulterated fear. Unfortunately, politicians, religions, and the nightly news are usually more interested in spinning fear to their advantage than they are in dispelling it.

A corporation, like the one in my fictional coffee commercial, usually seeks to attract customers and gain our allegiance by presenting an image of the good life that lures and compels us. With this technique, fear is not the driving force but more of the subtext. In other words, we might 'fear' the good life we are missing out on or 'fear' not keeping up with the Joneses.

In the case of politicians and the nightly news, however, fear is at the forefront. Every election cycle the fangs come out. Sometimes it seems like the only reason to vote on X is because of the crippling dread of what will happen if we don't. Surely the whole world will fall apart and be run over by evil unless we vote "no" on Prop Terrified!

The nightly news is an orgy of fear. The occasional heart-warming "human interest story" merely serves to amplify our sense of the goodness being threatened on all sides. My personal favorite news moments are the "health" segments

---

[8] Franklin D. Roosevelt's 1932 Inaugural Address.

where medical experts educate us about insidious diseases we had theretofore no reason to be afraid of.   Once informed, we can allow fear to roll like a mighty river.

If the nightly news is an orgy of fear, *The Colbert Report* is the unleashing of a Fear Apocalypse.   Segments like the "Threat Down," "Who's Attacking Me Now?," and "The Enemy Within" are only the most obvious elements in Colbert's parody of TV punditry which delight simultaneously in exuding personal confidence while spreading fear like Tinkerbell spreads fairy dust.

Asked exactly what his character was concerned with making America afraid of Colbert answered emphatically, "Everything!"[9]

Sowing fear, of course, is evil.   This is precisely the point the parody attempts to make.   To spread and inflate fear is to purposefully turn people away from God in the sense that when God reveals Godself the words are always, "Fear not! Be not afraid!"[10]

"Why is fear so intoxicating?" Colbert was asked in an interview.

"I suppose fear is like a drug. A little bit isn't that bad, but you can get addicted to the consumption and distribution of it. What's evil is the purposeful distribution of fear...   If you're injecting fear into other people, then you're trying to kill their

---

[9] "The Playboy Interview: Stephen Colbert on Politics, Grief and Bill O'Reilly" by Eric Spitznagel, originally published in *Playboy*, November 2012, posted online April 10, 2014.   URL: http://playboysfw.kinja.com/the-playboy-interview-stephen-colbert-on-politics-gri-1561831379

[10] For example: Luke 1:13; 30; 2:10

minds. You're trying to get them to stop thinking. That's antithetical to the founding of this country. It's on the Jefferson Memorial. I'm stealing this from Jefferson, but I'm also stealing it from the movie Born Yesterday. Bill Holden takes Judy Holliday to the Jefferson Memorial, and they read the inscription together. 'I have sworn upon the altar of God eternal hostility against every form of tyranny over the mind of man.' Fear is an attempt to impose tyranny over someone's mind. It's an act of oppression."[11]

Fear aims at protecting life, but it also refuses to acknowledge that death is often the pathway to life.   In fact, if resurrection life is the kind of "good life" we are aiming for, death is the *only* pathway to life.   But what's true metaphysically can also be experienced in "the little things."   Like the metaphoric death of "bombing" on stage as a comedian which, once endured, leads to life and fearlessness.   Once you realize you can endure such death and find life on the other side it enables you to do more, to risk more, to aim higher.

It is certainly *not* the case that what doesn't kill you makes you stronger.   We all move closer to death with every passing day. Nevertheless, this mistaken insight probably comes from the experience and realization that the deaths we undergo (trials, sufferings, grief) do not have to have the last word.   There can be life on the other side.

---

[11] "The Playboy Interview: Stephen Colbert on Politics, Grief and Bill O'Reilly" by Eric Spitznagel, originally published in *Playboy*, November 2012, posted online April 10, 2014.   URL: http://playboysfw.kinja.com/the-playboy-interview-stephen-colbert-on-politics-gri-1561831379

Jesus said something similar about wheat stalks. "Unless a kernel of wheat falls to the ground and dies, it remains a single seed.   But if it dies it produces many seeds."[12]

He was actually talking about something much bigger. Namely, the gospel itself, and that in Christ death does not have the last word.   Life has the last word.   Here is the source of all hope and the wellspring of joy:

"Anyone who loves their life will lose it, while anyone who hates their life in this world will keep it for eternal life."[13]

The fact remains that death is the prerequisite for resurrection life.   You can't have a resurrected body without first submitting a corpse.   Submitting that corpse, meanwhile, involves an active trust that death will not have the last word. Letting go, surrendering, and laying down one's life takes a great deal of courage.   Courage that is predicated on hope.

If fear is always fear of death, hope is always hope in God (or, at least, *someone* or *something* greater) because hope is deeper and bigger than mere optimism.   Colbert acknowledged. "Optimism is evidence based," as in, 'Based on the evidence I believe that things are going to work out fine.'"[14]   Hope involves bold trust irrespective of the evidence.   It's the belief in resurrection out of death.

In his first appearance on *The Colbert Report*, Corncl West was humorously subjected to antagonization by Colbert.   West

---

[12] John 12:24, *The New International Version*. (2011). Grand Rapids, MI: Zondervan.
[13] John 12:25, *The New International Version*. (2011). Grand Rapids, MI: Zondervan.
[14] Episode 823, aired January 18, 2011.

got worked up, declaring, "Hope is such a precious thing. We need courage, we need compassion, and we need hope."

West argued that these are precisely the conditions necessary to make for greatness in human life. As Martin Luther King, Jr. said, "If you have never found something so dear and precious that you aren't willing to die for it then you aren't fit to live."[15]

This is the zero point.

The meaning of life is embracing courage, rejecting fear, learning how to die, leaning on hope, and finding joy. This has fundamentally been the argument of these pages. Comedy, even the comedy of Stephen Colbert, can be a vehicle for engaging this gospel. Through laughter confront our fears and false constructions, especially our false constructions of God or in the name of God. We can face the truth even when it leads to dying because our hope is in the One who defeated death.

The gospel rejects fear and empties it of its power. Fear of speaking truth to power, fear of losing credibility or respectability, fear of our religious constructions, fear of God, fear of death, fear of condemnation. All are reduced to naught in the cross and empty tomb leaving behind only joy and freedom. Laughter helps us with the courage to let go.

---

[15] "But If Not" Sermon by Martin Luther King, Jr. delivered on November 5, 1967 at Ebenezer Baptist Church in Atlanta, Georgia. URL: https://www.youtube.com/watch?v=pOjpalO2seY&t=18m26s

Again, Colbert said it well, "It is impossible to laugh and be afraid at the same time. That is not a philosophical argument that is a physiological argument."[16]

LAST SEGMENT

On October 26, 2009 Cornel West sat across from Stephen Colbert in his familiar black suit. "Grave clothes" is how describes his usual attire.[17] This was his second of three appearances on *The Colbert Report*.

"Every human being is precious and priceless and is a brother or sister of mine because their body will one day be the culinary delight of terrestrial worms and I sympathize with them. So I want to be in solidarity with them, my brother, no matter what color no matter what culture, no matter what civilization…"

Colbert interrupted, "Because we're all gonna die!"

West continued, "Not only that but we're struggling for meaning and love in the short time that we're here. There is a death sentence inside time and space; no one of us gets out of time space alive."[18]

---

[16] On *Meet the Press* with David Gregory on NBC, published October 14, 2012. URL:
http://www.nbcnews.com/video/meet-the-press/49407301
[17] *"I Want To Be Like Jesus"* by Lisa Miller, May 6, 2012, New York Times Magazine, URL:
http://nymag.com/news/features/cornel-west-2012-5/index5.html
[18] Episode 626, aired October 26, 2009

No matter how I struggle and strive, I'll never get out of this world alive.   But hope is weightier than optimism, and joy is better than happiness.   Joy fuels hope for the future and allows us to laugh in the present, even as we prepare for death.

12.

Surprise

"Jesus himself stood among them and said to them, "Peace be with you."

They were startled and terrified

Luke 24:36-37[1]

OPENING WORDS

"We're not here to frost cupcakes, we're not here to pussy foot around... It's time to drive the eighteen wheeler of truth down the throats of our enemies!"[2]

"Duck, duck, duck... Truth! This is *The Colbert Report!*"[3]

"Warmth is to sun as truth is to me."[4]

---

[1] Luke 24:36-37, *The New International Version*. (2011). Grand Rapids, MI: Zondervan.
[2] Episode 1371, aired June 24, 2014
[3] Episode 389, aired April 30, 2008
[4] Episode 66, aired March 15, 2006

"Watch this show in a well ventilated area. My truth can be overpowering."[5]

"You've heard of truth in advertising? This is truth *with* advertising."[6]

"That tingling sensation? It means the truth is working."[7]

"You might want to add water because this show is concentrated truth."[8]

"Open wide, baby bird, because mama's got a big, fat night crawler of truth."[9]

"The truth hurts. Fortunately for America, I'm a masochist."[10]

"I got 99 problems but the truth ain't one."[11]

"Frère Jacques, Frère Jacques, Dormez-truth. This is *The Colbert Report!*"[12]

These are the sorts of phrases that introduce the show. What follows them far from true.

In fact, phrases like these are the signal, warning, and announcement that fakery, buffoonery, and falsehood are about to ensue. The more passionately and earnestly Stephen Colbert insists what he is saying is right, the more any sane or

---

[5] Episode 260, aired May 16, 2007
[6] Episode 279, aired June 26, 2007
[7] Episode 296, aired August 9, 2007
[8] Episode 326, aired October 17, 2007
[9] Episode 1, aired October 17, 2005
[10] Episode 24, aired January 10, 2006
[11] Episode 25, aired January 11, 2006
[12] Episode 429, aired July 31, 2008

discerning viewer should suspect what is being represented as neither factual nor actual.

Deliberate engagement of foolishness and falsehood is not "just" for laughs in the sense that it is futile or meaningless.   It is not nihilistic or apathetic.   At its best it is hopeful rather than cynical.   Satire is ridiculous but not absurd.   It is lying in the service of honesty, truthiness for the sake of truth.

Comedy is a servant of truth, but it is not truth embodied.

Comedy's first aim is not to answer questions but raise questions.   In doing so it makes way for truth and creates space for considering new, better, and deeper answers.   Don't look to comedians for answers but to tease out what needs answering.

A comic serves the truth much like a court jester served the kingdom or a prophet serves the people.

The court jester was not the law maker or "The Decider" but the one commissioned to expose the truth behind politicking.

The prophet is not the leader but the one who calls a spade a spade and urges people toward justice, love, and truth.

Comedy takes our assumptions, the way we do things in this world, the hypocrisies we comfortably overlook and reflects them back at us like a mirror.   Technically speaking, comedy's first move is always negative (or deconstructive) because it takes something we think or know and says, "Not so fast!"

Rather than giving us a firm footing, it destabilizes the ground beneath us.

WHALES AGAIN

At the heart of every joke is surprise. A punchline gets laughs because you didn't see it coming. Good comics draw their audience in to a story, build up expectations of what should happen next, and then deliver a surprise of something unexpected.

A routine example might be the whale song joke discussed earlier. In this sketch comedy bit, a folk singer comes on stage and announces she is going to do a song for the whales. She draws the audience in to believe the narrative. While tuning her guitar she talks about her love of the earth and empathy for disadvantaged species.

The comic carries on long enough for the audience to *believe* her as an earth-conscious folk artist to the point that they *expect* her to deliver her best work in the vein of Peter, Paul, and Mary. The surprise arrives when, instead, she blurts out crazy and awful sounding animal noises mimicking underwater whale communication. The expectation is a song for the whales by a folk singer. Delivered in its place is a whale song by a wingnut.

This joke is not high art. And the surest way to empty a joke of humor is to analyze it or explain how it works. Nevertheless, the way this one stupid joke functions with respect to surprise is analogous to comedy as a whole. As Colbert observed, the whale joke works every time.[13] The reason is expectation and surprise.

---

[13] *A.D.D. Comedy Podcast with Dave Razowsky and Ian Foley*, November 20, 2012, interview with Stephen Colbert

SURPRISE

The dynamic of expectation and surprise is critical to the function of comedy even when you know the punchline. If you are hearing a joke for the twelfth time, if you are listening to a variation on a well-used formula… this dynamic is always present. You are led along in one direction until the surprise is introduced moving in the opposite direction.

Variations abound. Satire can even reverse the dynamic of expectation and surprise. For example, when Colbert is interviewing someone he regularly acts completely oblivious to the implications of what the guest is saying. When a guest raises a challenging point, Colbert maintains his consistent ignorance such that he only hears it as an affirmation of his impenetrable, narrow worldview.

The "expectation" being built up is the expectation we would have of any rational person in normal conversation. Namely, we'd naturally expect Colbert to respond to what a guest is attempting to communicate. His willful ignorance is the "surprise" that never gets old. The delightful ongoing "surprise" of *The Colbert Report* is that Colbert's character never admits failure, defeat, or entertains the possibility of altering or amending his point of view.

A specific instance of this dynamic was Colbert's interview with Cornel West in 2011. When West said, "There is joy in serving others," Colbert responded, "I take joy in others serving me… You need to go to better restaurants!"

When Colbert argued that social justice should be the domain of churches as opposed to government West said he would love to see "our churches on fire for justice." Colbert was aghast, "You want to burn our churches! What a horrible thing to say!"

The more extreme Colbert's refusal to meaningfully engage with the substance of the issues that confront him, the funnier it gets. When a guest says something profound that garners applause from the audience, Colbert's plays on the assumption that the clapping is an affirmation of his disagreement, rage, or interviewing skill.

The comedy enlarges in proportion with Colbert's ignorance. The more blatant his misunderstanding of the obvious, the more we laugh. Colbert's ignorance and pride are surprise in the sense that they are breeches from normality. Viewers expect the unexpected from Stephen Colbert in the sense that no one is actually shocked. But those two elements of expectation and surprise function in conversation (or dialectic) to make the comedy work.

It doesn't matter if the surprise is subtle or literally surprising at all. The unexpected can be expected. But expectation and surprise are still the lynch pins of comedy.

ASSUMPTIONS

Surprise is an inexhaustible resource for comedy because there will always be expectations and "norms" to exploit and undermine. Human beings are full of assumptions so challenging assumptions is always possible.

When an assumption we've held gets hit with a surprise attack, anger is an option, but so is laughter. There is a popular lexical adage that says when we "assume" it makes something-less-than-flattering out of you and me (or "u" and "me").   In other words, assumptions are weak spots ripe for comical pillaging.

On the other hand, we could hardly live, move, and have our being in this world if we didn't regularly make assumptions.   I assume, for example, a set of atmospheric conditions such that when I step out my front door I will not fly off into space like if my house was located on the moon.   I also assume when I go to sleep at night that I will wake up the next morning.   I assume that I'm more likely to be wrong about the latter then the former.   Still, I like my chances and carry on with my assumptions.

We can't escape assumptions and we wouldn't want to. Science tells us, for example, that our brains have an incredible capacity to take in our surroundings in "real time" because of assumptions.   For example, if you regularly mountain bike down harrowing forest trails at breakneck speed your previous experience and knowledge is etched into your neurological framework such that you can make assumptions about the present and make split second decisions faster than you could if you had to rationally consider data and make conscious and deliberated choices while riding.

Many optical illusions work the same way.   You see something, your brain detects a pattern from previous experience, and your brain "fills in" the missing data.   I once had a friend who shaved off half his beard but it took his family members before they noticed.   They saw the half beard and mentally "filled in the rest."   Assumptions can help us or mislead us.

INTERPRETATION

In every moment of our lives we experience phenomena (sights, sounds, conversations, emotions). We receive sights and experiences. We read and are taught. Whatever senses we have the good fortune to be blessed with, we employ them to engage with the universe around us.

We consider and decide. Somehow, someway, we fit all of this into a grid of understanding. We form and develop a perspective, an outlook, a worldview. Included in this, of course, is a set of assumptions. Stuff we can count on. Like gravity.

But phenomena (stuff we encounter by various means) is always interpreted. We hear a sound overhead and look up to identify the object as a plane. How do we know it is a plane? On the one hand, we can't know with absolute certainty. On the other hand, its location, its noise, its shape, our experiences, and our assumptions lead us to say, "It's not a bird or superman I just saw. That was a plane."

Surprise comes when something doesn't fit our understanding.

If we hear a sound overhead and look up to see a flying boat we would be surprised (and probably laugh out loud). A flying boat does not fit our experiences and violates our assumptions. Such a sight would probably cause us to go back and reconsider everything we thought we knew about aerodynamics, gravity, and previous experience with boats, sky, and flying objects. More likely still, we might conclude that we'd eaten some bad pizza, had a hallucination, and chalk up the whole episode as a brief psychiatric break.

Surprise happens when a hole is poked in our understanding. Surprise occurs when we experience something that doesn't fit with how we understand the world which causes us to question and modify that understanding.

Surprise is saying, "Oh!   So it's not like I thought it was" and going back to address or reshape our worldview.

NARRATIVE

Another word for our understanding, wealth of experience, and set of assumptions is "narrative" or "story."   We're not computers or transcendent analytical observers but human beings ensconced in time and place with parents and bodies and particular genetic make-ups.   We all have particular stories.   Our stories or narratives are how we understand our lives, our world, the universe, and all of existence fitting together (or not fitting together).   Our narratives can have holes and unknowns of every sort.   Regardless, everyone has a narrative in the sense that everyone has a perspective or a worldview.

Narratives are important to acknowledge. There are bucket loads of competing narratives the whole world around – some comprehensive and some very much less so.   Everyone who speaks, speaks from a perspective and story complete with assumptions, and often, allegiance to a larger story.

That larger story can be political, scientific, or religious. Religions provide meta-narratives (big stories) in the sense that they provide an account for the meaning of life, the ground of being, the human condition, and the ultimate goal of all things.

They tell a big story and invite adherents to fit their personal narratives and stories into that grand story. Political narratives, cultural narratives, and personal narratives function in the same way. Narratives order some part of the universe and invite us to accept their version of reality as true and correct.

A person can confirm this with a very simple experiment:

First, identify a global conflict or situation in the world characterized by frequent violence. Sadly, there are many to choose from.

Second, observe how different news sources cover the story. What do they report as the background of the conflict? Who is involved? What bits of information are chosen and deemed newsworthy? What bits are left out? And how is the information intended shape understanding of the situation?

With these two steps, a person should be able to identify a larger story or narrative that is implied or explicitly laid out. The last step is to compare these stories with one another.

In America, the coverage is very different on MSNC than it is on Fox News, which is different again from CNN. Regardless of the network, an observable narrative almost always emerges. Particular words and phrases are chosen and consciously repeated to aid the forming of a narrative for understanding events being reported on.

This little experiment is interesting when carried out locally, but it becomes fascinating if an observer goes the extra mile and looks at how stories are told by news organizations in Israel, Palestine, Egypt, Iran, Kenya, Pakistan, Russia, and other non-US sources.   Organizations all claiming to represent truth and professing a commitment to objectivity can nevertheless radically contradict one another.

Narrative matters.

It is impossible to look at the world without being located. We are bound in space and time and our own stories from which we look at the world around us.

You can't divorce yourself from your own interpretive lens, your experiences, your assumptions, your narrative.   This is not to say we can's affirm the rightness of some narratives and the wrongness of others.   Still, the recognition that we are located in particular stories as opposed to embodiments of universal reality should give us pause and just a little bit of humility.   I heard it put recently; no one has a "God's eye view" of reality.   When we attempt to speak or act as if we do, all manner of trouble ensues.

DON'T POKE THE BEAR

Comedy exists to poke at narratives.   In fact that's pretty much the only thing it does.   Whether it is benign assumptions (like that folk singers sing folk songs) or deeply held religious or political beliefs, it is the challenge levied against our assumptions that makes something funny. Expectation countered with surprise.

Satire is how assumptions are challenged on *The Colbert Report*. Stephen Colbert takes a position, and by doing so undermines it.   If Stephen Colbert or his writers see some narrative on the nightly news they perceive as false or wrong, the classical move is to single out that wrong perspective and embrace it wholeheartedly and exaggeratedly. The effect is to challenge the credibility of the original news piece. In essence, "Are things really the way you portray them?"

Comedy casts doubts, asks questions, and subverts narratives.

The surprise dynamic applies to meaningless jokes as much as it does to serious comedy. It is even the logic behind physical comedy. When Dad pitches a softball to his son or daughter, you don't expect the kid to bat the ball straight into his groin. At least, Dad certainly didn't expect it! That's what makes it funny.

This "surprise is the secret of success for shows like *America's Funniest Home Videos.* But for meaningful comedy or "jokes that matter" it is much more profound. We all have our stories, assumptions, and ways of fitting things together. We also all have our biases, our self-preserving justifications for our own shortcomings, our own ways of preferencing our desires at the expense of others, our own mechanisms for protecting our comfort and security, our own ways of carving up the world into "us" and "them."

Enter comedy. Enter surprise. Comedy doesn't build narratives or structures of meaning, it tears them down. Comedy takes our expectations and assumptions and says, "The firm ground you count on is not as firm as you think."

Comedy is supposed to be offensive. It is designed to make us question what we thought we could count on. That is the very nature of surprise and the base ingredient for generating laughter. At the same time, laughter is the medicine that enables us to handle the trauma of our stereotypes and assumptions being broken.

This is the way that comedy makes way for truth. It subverts our assumptions and breaks down our narratives but leaves us with joy so we can build something new and better at the site of our wreckage.

AND MORE

Comedians, court jesters, and prophets can subvert narratives to make room for truth. If they're funny they can aid their deconstruction with an injection of joy. But the function of comedy can also be sacred.

If I hear a noise above, I look up expecting to see a plane. If I see a boat, I would be surprised, I would probably laugh, and I would go on and try to reconcile my experience with my narrative understanding of the world.

But what if I saw something I had no category for? No experience of? What if I encountered something I had no analogous understanding of whatsoever?

If I reported that I saw a flying Spaghetti monster, it would certainly be unusual and probably not believable. But that claim still invokes categories that belong to the world of accepted assumptions and the world of the known. Spaghetti, flying, and the mythical idea of monsters are all known concepts.

But what if I encountered something Other?

This, of course, is the domain of God, the Holy Spirit, and religious faith. Encounter, event, and Otherness causing rupture in our constructions of existence is at the heart of Christianity. The death and resurrection of Jesus is referred to by many as "event" in precisely this sense.

"Behold," said Jesus, "I am making all things new."[14]

For that newness to take effect, we have to let go of the old stuff. Which includes our assumptions and expectations.

On *The Colbert Report* in 2011, Father Jim Martin (official "Chaplain of the Colbert Nation") claimed that laughter is at the heart of the spiritual life.[15]

He pointed to the birth of Isaac recorded in Genesis which involved Abraham laughing, Sarah laughing, and the child of promise being named Isaac which in Hebrew means "he laughs." Martin observed, "You could say that the three great monotheistic religions began with a laugh."

"Wow," Colbert responded thoughtfully and impressed. He then offered, "They don't giggle much together, though."

If the Christian religion began with a laugh, in an oblique sense, it also culminates with one. If the formula at the heart of comedy involves expectations being subverted by surprise, there is no better joke than the expectation of death having the last word getting toppled by the surprise punchline of resurrection. Laugh or don't laugh, but when we allow comedy to poke and prod at our assumptions, we put ourselves

---

[14] Revelation 21:5
[15] Episode 957, aired November 9, 2011

where we might encounter something good, something true, and someone Other.

"Knock knock. Who's there? The truth. No joke."[16]

---

[16] Episode 23, aired November 30, 2005

13.

Conclusion

"Truly I tell you, unless you change and become like little children,
you will never enter the kingdom of heaven."

Matthew 18:3[1]

SUNDAY SCHOOL

In 2008, Dr. Phillip Zimbardo was on *The Colbert Report*
promoting his book *The Lucifer Effect.* Zimbardo laid out his
argument lucidly and effectively saying good people should
evaluate authority because authority can convince good people
to do bad things.

Things were fine until Zimbardo cast his theory about the
ambiguity between good and evil and pointed the metaphysical
finger of blame at God.

---

[1] *The New International Version*. (2011). Grand Rapids, MI: Zondervan.

Zimbardo's reading of the biblical story of humanity's "Fall from Grace" was a bet between God and Lucifer about whether or not Adam, the human, was corruptible. Because the human sinned, Zimbardo reasoned, "Lucifer was right and God was wrong."[2]

When Zimbardo uttered those words they hit Colbert's character like a shockwave and possibly had a similar impact on the man behind the mask.

The host reeled back in disbelief. Zimbardo took the opportunity to continue.

"If God was into reconciliation, he would have said 'I made a mistake.' God created hell. Paradoxically, it was God who created Hell as a place to put Lucifer and the fallen angels, and had he not created Hell, then evil would not exist."

Colbert's quick wit kicked in and he retorted with a rapid-fire theological sequence to counter Zimbardo:

"Evil exists because of the disobedience of Satan. God gave Satan, the angels, and man, free will; Satan used his free will and abused it by not obeying authority; Hell was created by Satan's disobedience to God and his purposeful removal from God's love, which is what Hell *is* – removing yourself from God's love. You send yourself to Hell. God does not send you there!"

Colbert's words were cadenced and confident. At the conclusion of his mini-rant the audience responded with whistles, shouts, and applause for Stephen Colbert.

---

[2] Episode 352, aired February 11, 2008

Zimbardo answered dismissively, "Obviously you learned well in Sunday School."

Colbert hit him with the knockout punch shouting, "I teach Sunday School, motherf****r."

Zimbardo was speechless. Colbert started to laugh as though he shocked himself. The audience roared ecstatically and the interview was over.

MESSIAH COMPLEX

Perhaps you think I've made too much of Stephen Colbert and gone too far in painting him as an esteemed cultural critic or prophetic voice crying in the wilderness for the sake of truth.

Maybe I've been describing him as messianic :

Stephen Colbert has born the cross of becoming an idiot, public spectacle, and fool for the sake of any and all who would notice or take heed. Forsaking respectability, not considering his imagined self-importance or dignity something to be grasped, he let go of any pretension making way for us to have joy and hope by bearing witness to the truth.

Stephen Colbert is not the Messiah. He is a comedian who has said of himself that he is quite happy to send his kids to college on poop jokes.

I said at the beginning, *Telling the Truthiness* is not about Stephen Colbert. It's about you, and me, and whoever has ears to hear. The question is not whether Stephen Colbert is a Christian. The question is who are *you?*

Gospel, literally, means good news. In its purest usage, the word gospel is good news having to do with the person of Jesus. For seekers on this journey of life, I believe that in the comedic craft of Stephen Colbert on *The Colbert Report* – gospel abounds. Through comedy, humor, satire, and laughter – Jesus is present, too. Present to be enjoyed if our ears and eyes are open.

When I look at Jesus I see a commitment to truth – a truth that shines to expose hypocrisies as well as false narratives about enemies, about God and about ourselves. I see a willingness to speak truth to power, to experience shame, to lose friends, to go to the cross.

In Jesus I hear a summons to accept all as gift, even our sufferings, because if we are joined with him in his suffering how much more will we be participants in his forever living life? In Jesus I hear a call to surrender my credibility and pride, to surrender and come clean as the fool I am and live in his life instead of my own.

When I look at Jesus I see mercy, compassion, and love that beckon us to intimacy with God, living in Jesus' own relationship with his Father. Jesus is the one who reveals God's love and mercy and desire to give life.

When I look at Jesus I see a new way of being, a mode of existence initialized where there is nothing to fear and all that remains is pure freedom. When I look at Jesus I see that I can be authentic, happy, sad, smart, or confused. I see that I can approach the throne and speak, wonder, laugh, joke, and seek answers – because everything is grace and condemnation has been removed from the future and put into the past.

When I look at Jesus I see the love of God.   But even when I can't see at all and everything looks like darkness that "love that will not let me go" has a hold of me and I have joy and peace.

This makes me smile. Because joy is always a surprise running counter to my dour expectations. For me, watching *The Colbert Report* can be a near-sacramental experience of this free, fearless, and fun ethos of living in parrhesia. That's gospel.

THE JOY MACHINE

Stephen Colbert was taught as an improv actor that the number one rule is to say "yes" to everything.   If the actors are told on stage, "You are doctors," they accept it.

"Yes.   We are doctors."

And then they build on it.   "You are in an ice cave."

"Yes.   We are doctors in an ice cave."

Colbert explained, "To build a scene, you have to accept. To build anything onstage, you have to accept what the other improviser initiates on stage.[3]"

This way of being allows for joy but it also makes space to accept suffering, failure, and wrong turns.

---

[3] 2006 Commencement speech by Stephen Colbert delivered at Knox College, Galesburg, IL (specific example of "doctors in ice caves" from this same speech).   URL:
http://departments.knox.edu/newsarchive/news_events/2006/x12547.html

"One of the things that I like about improvisation is that, literally, there are no mistakes. There are only opportunities."[4]

Colbert went on to explain that you revel in the goodness created by comedy but you also embrace whatever goes wrong. "You embrace the bomb. And that idea is so appealing to me, because it's also about valuing suffering, and gratitude for bad things — because really, what's the option? Mother Theresa said, "Smile and accept." I love that."[5]

Saying "yes," fearlessly embracing the role of the fool, risking credibility, and putting it all out there is inarguably the secret of Stephen Colbert's success if there ever was one. His grandmother advised him early on, "Never refuse a legitimate adventure!" Then, parenthetically, she added, "and it's up to you to figure out what legitimate means."[6]

When Stephen Colbert accepted the job to take the place of David Letterman and bring *The Colbert Report* to a close at the end of its ninth year, the social media opinion-sphere lit up. The comedic genius of Stephen Colbert has been undeniably connected with his creation and embodiment of a character. The over-the-top mock pundit is the one who has won over hearts and minds, gaining fans in high and low places. Even on *The Daily Show* it was the poorly informed, high status idiot that "killed" night after night.

---

[4] "Stephen Colbert Web Exclusive" in *Parade* online from interview with James Kaplan.   URL:
http://parade.condenast.com/50118/parade/stephen-colbert-web-excl
usive/
[5] Ibid.
[6] "Stephen Colbert: 'arch conservative'", Rebecca Ascher Walsh, *Los Angeles Times*, June 1, 2009. URL:
http://articles.latimes.com/2009/jun/01/news/en-colbert1

With thicker framed glasses, a more genuine tone, and a more reverent audience… Will Stephen Colbert find a new comedic voice?   Will he shine on the stage of network television like he did at Comedy Central?   Will he be up for the task of creating a new template for a new television show?   Will he continue to take risks?   What if it falls flat?

Once again, parrhesia should be invoked.

It's not, as Stephen Colbert claimed on *The Daily Show with Jon Stewart*, that Colbert has "won television" and is now moving on to new conquests.   It *is*, however, that there is nothing to fear.   Whatever happens, how could Stephen Colbert not heed the words of his grandmother and refuse a legitimate adventure?

Even if the new *Late Night* bombs, I'll be watching – looking and listening for Good News.   Colbert himself said it best: "Will saying "yes" get you in trouble at times?   Will saying "yes" lead you to doing some foolish things?   Yes it will. But don't be afraid to be a fool…   Cynicism is a self-imposed blindness, a rejection of the world because we are afraid it will hurt us or disappoint us. Cynics always say "no." But saying "yes" begins things. Saying "yes" is how things grow. Saying "yes" leads to knowledge… As long as you have the strength to… Say "yes.""[7]

---

[7] 2006 Commencement speech by Stephen Colbert delivered at Knox College, Galesburg, IL URL:
http://departments.knox.edu/newsarchive/news_events/2006/x12547.html

38042500R00129

Made in the USA
Lexington, KY
19 December 2014